# THEY'RE WATCHING YOU!
## The Age of Surveillance
### by Tony Lesce

Breakout Productions
Port Townsend, Washington

*This book is sold for informational purposes only. Neither the author nor the publisher will be held accountable for the use or misuse of the information contained in this book.*

**They're Watching You!** The Age of Surveillance
© 1998 by Tony Lesce

All rights reserved. No part of this book may be reproduced or stored in any form whatsoever without the prior written consent of the publisher. Reviews may quote brief passages without the written consent of the publisher as long as proper credit is given.

**Published by:**
Breakout Productions
PO Box 1643
Port Townsend, WA 98368

Cover illustration by Mary Fleener
Photographs by Tony Lesce

**ISBN 0-9666932-2-1**
**Library of Congress Card Catalog 98-87561**

# Contents

**Introduction** ............................................. 1

**Chapter One**
Surveillance in Fiction ............................... 5

**Chapter Two**
Private and Public Surveillance ................. 11

**Chapter Three**
Surveillance as Intimidation ...................... 33

**Chapter Four**
Digging Up Dirt ........................................ 45

**Chapter Five**
Commercial Motives ................................. 49

**Chapter Six**
The Myth of "Security" ............................. 57

**Chapter Seven**
Investigations ............................................ 71

**Chapter Eight**
Tools and Techniques ............................... 75

**Chapter Nine**
The Internet ............................................ 107

**Chapter Ten**
　　Protecting Yourself ......................................... 111
**Chapter Eleven**
　　The Future ..................................................... 129

# Introduction

They're watching you, sometimes without your knowledge, and almost always without your consent. Who are "they?" Not only, as many people believe, the government and its various agencies, but private agencies and companies as well. You're being watched, not only by the "Big Brother" of government, but by many "Little Brothers" who have a burning interest in what you do, think, and feel.

The shocking death of Britain's Princess Diana was a wake-up call to everyone concerned about the abuses of surveillance, especially as practiced flagrantly and often illegally by private parties. As a celebrity, Diana was under the constant scrutiny of camera-armed freelance photographers elbowing to try to catch a photo of her swimming nude or kissing a boyfriend. Fortunately, most of us aren't newsworthy enough to become targets of these "paparazzi," but we're still the targets of more casual surveillance, which is the theme of this book.

Surveillance is obvious to any American who spends a normal day at work, shopping, or enjoying leisure activities. Go to a supermarket and the signs of

# They're Watching You!
## The Age of Surveillance

unrelenting surveillance are evident in the black domes suspended from the ceilings. Withdraw money from an automatic teller machine (ATM) and you see the eye of a video camera peering at you throughout the transaction. Go into a bank and you'll see TV cameras out in the open, recording everyone within their fields of view. In most places, surveillance is not as oppressive as that described in George Orwell's novel *1984*. However, at airports, surveillance is especially heavy-handed, with barriers, metal detector gates, and uniformed "security guards" as well as police.

There is in this country (and in many others as well) a "fear industry" promoting "security," allegedly providing protection against a variety of threats, some of which are real, and others which are chimerical. Private security is a bigger business than the official police, and private security guards outnumber official police by well over two to one. The private security budget is one and one-half times as great as that spent on official police, and provides a profitable business for the companies engaged in it. In the process, private security encroaches on our rights, and invades our privacy, all in the name of protecting us.

The fear industry works hand-in-hand with the "controllers," officials on a power trip, who enjoy imposing rules and restrictions on other people. There have always been controllers, people who sought positions of authority, but those of previous eras had to work with primitive tools. They lacked the technological marvels of today, which make total control of people's lives possible.

*Introduction*

Today's technological tools are neutral. They can serve for good or evil, depending on the individuals using them. Formerly, a prison required iron bars and stone walls. Today, an electronic prison confines its captives, often without their even realizing that they are not free.

# Chapter One
# Surveillance in Fiction

The surprising trend in fictional accounts of electronic surveillance is how closely these parallel real life, showing an increasing sophistication regarding tools and techniques, and more importantly, who is carrying out the surveillance. Ever since the invention of telephone wiretapping during the 1890s, there have been fictional accounts, most in the hard-boiled private detective genre, and most of these have been inaccurate. The authors of these masterpieces often disregard the legalities, which, if violated by a real-life private detective, would open him up to prosecution.

Some fictional accounts have described wiretapping by government agencies. One of the best is Frederick Forsyth's *Day of the Jackal,* which appeared in its Viking edition in 1971 and its Bantam paperback in 1972. The basic plot is that a professional assassin is out to kill France's President de Gaulle, and the novel describes the progress he makes toward his objective while a harried and overworked French police commissar tries to stop him.

The Jackal always seems to be one step ahead of the police, and escapes minutes before police arrive to apprehend him. Each time it's the day after Commissar

**They're Watching You!**
The Age Of Surveillance

Lebel, who's in charge of the case, delivers his nightly briefing to government officials. This frustrates and baffles the commissar, and he reasons that the Jackal must be receiving inside information. He orders taps placed on the telephones of everybody who attends the nightly meetings at the Ministry of Justice. A few hours after he orders the taps placed, the technicians notify him that they have a tape of a suspicious conversation. After listening to it, he realizes that an army colonel attached to the President's office has been leaking details of the investigation to his mistress, who in turn relays the information to a contact in the anti-de Gaulle underground.[1]

We see the surveillance theme best in Hollywood films, the majority of which are garbage, but with some fairly good pieces of work here and there.

One of the earliest films with electronic surveillance as its major theme was *The Anderson Tapes*, starring Sean Connery. This 1971 film, based on Lawrence Sanders' novel, depicts how a convict, just released from prison after serving his time, remains constantly under surveillance by one government agency or other. In the bus station, New York Port Authority Police use closed-circuit TV (CCTV) cameras to monitor the various corridors, waiting rooms, escalators, and other public areas. The main character's various contacts and acquaintances, directly or tangentially connected to organized crime, are therefore under police or federal surveillance. The film also depicts audio and visual surveillance by private parties as well. A private detective uses audio bugs to monitor the ex-con's girlfriend's apartment, hired by her jealous former boyfriend. When the ex-con and his gang carry out the robbery of an upscale apartment house that is the main purpose of his efforts, they are under surveillance by several closed-circuit cameras connected to monitors on the desk of the security guard in the lobby.

Even then, there was awareness that much surveillance was illegal. At the end of the film, after the robbers are captured or killed by police, the scene jumps from one government office to another, showing how agents quickly erase surveillance tapes to destroy the evidence that electronic monitoring ever took place.

In 1974 came *The Parallax View*, based on Loren Singer's novel of the same title. The plot was that a malignant and sinister arm of the U.S. Government pursued the hero, who barely managed to remain ahead of them during the film, until his eventual demise. The clandestine government agency tracked his uses of credit cards via computer and kept on his heels throughout the film.

*Sliver*, a 1993 film starring Sharon Stone, is perhaps the most realistic and most relevant to our modern era. Sharon Stone moves into an upscale apartment house where the owner has installed a very comprehensive closed-circuit array that covers literally every room in every apartment, including all bathrooms. The purpose is not security, in this case, but rather to satisfy the owner's voyeuristic bent, as he enjoys snooping into the lives of his tenants.

About half-way through the film, he confesses to Sharon Stone that he is the owner, not merely another tenant as he'd pretended to be, and shows her his surveillance system. Telling her it cost him six million dollars, he demonstrates its functions to her, unaware that instead of being impressed, she's horrified. Although the film's plot is thin and the dialogue trite (the film's closing line is "Get a life.") the portrayal of how comprehensive modern surveillance can become is very true-to-life.

The most realistic aspect of *Sliver* is that the sinister, voyeuristic surveillance is being performed not by a noxious government agency, but by a free-wheeling private individual. As we'll see, most electronic surveillance in real life is by private individuals or agencies, undertaken in the name of "security."

A basic fact is the police are mostly a reactive force, responding to reported crimes and occasionally making an effort at "crime prevention." Crime prevention usually consists of advising citizens to lock their doors, be careful about admitting strangers, and call the police at once if they observe suspicious behavior. Very few officers conduct surveillance of known criminals because police agencies cannot spare the resources.

Federal agencies have more latitude. Free of the duty of patrolling the streets, they can indulge themselves and carry out more surveillances of those they deem suspicious. This is why, when a wire-tapping case occurs, the agency involved is likely to be the FBI, Secret Service, or a few other federal ones, including the Intelligence Division of the Department of Energy. This little-known bureau has more latitude than the high-profile FBI.

By far the most surveillances, legal and illegal, are by private parties, who may be employers, private investigative agencies, and their agents. We'll examine why and how in the following chapters.

**Notes:**

1. *Day of the Jackal*, Forsyth, Frederick, New York, Bantam, 1972, pp. 440-442.

# Chapter Two
# Private and Public Surveillance

As we've seen, surveillance is practiced by both public and private agencies. A primitive type of surveillance, the "mail cover," is a technique postal inspectors can use without a warrant to discover who sends and receives mail from whom. Private companies use "background checks" to investigate job applicants. After hiring, identity badges or cards allow access to the premises, and some models tell the employer's security officers exactly where each employee is in the plant every moment. It is literally possible to document exactly how many minutes and seconds an employee spends in the bathroom every day.

Private security is big business, employing about 1.5 million people with about a $52 billion budget.[1] This is significantly more than the personnel assigned to American official policing, who number only about 600,000 officers.

Police agencies have more important things to do than employ surveillance against people not suspected of any crime. However, private security agencies do exactly that. Private security and investigative agencies have no police powers. If they discover evidence of a crime, they're required by law to turn it over to the police and cooperate fully with official investigators.

## Workplace Surveillance

How do private investigative and guard agencies spend their time? Most of it involves checking out job applicants, carrying out surveillance of stores and factories to detect evidence of theft or other misbehavior on the job, and investigating employees who come under suspicion.

Workplace theft and workplace violence are the main excuses used to justify surveillance and investigation of employees. There are good reasons for this. One expert lists corporate culture, authoritarian management, and incompetent management as leading to workplace violence.[2]

As we'll see, employees are under direct surveillance in some companies. Cameras and other electronic means allow security guards to know where everyone is at every moment, even in the toilet. Employers are very concerned about employee theft. In retailing, employee theft accounts for greater losses than shoplifting. In other types of companies, employees steal items of varying value, from pens and pencils to computers and other high-dollar items.

Some employee theft is surprisingly hard to track. One employee in Virginia on business used his company's Federal Express account number to ship a personal purchase to his home in Connecticut.[3]

Long-distance telephone calls are another way for employees to steal from their employers. Employees frequently run up a lot of time calling friends several states away, and on company time to boot.[4]

Stealing time is the hardest to pin down. Extending coffee breaks and lunch periods is common, and although time clocks are a partial solution, realistically employees can punch another's card. This is a serious enough problem in some companies that management posts signs by each time clock, warning that punching another employee's card is cause for dismissal. While almost half of American workers steal tangible items such as pens, envelopes, and food, almost 60 percent steal time.[5]

A survey of the security concerns of major companies *(Fortune* 1000) by Pinkerton showed that employee theft is the number two concern among security directors, second only to workplace violence. The role of the Internet is obvious, and Pinkerton's publication points out that "surfing" the Internet during working hours is a common problem, which they categorize as "theft of time."[6]

This is why some employers are installing electronic security systems that track employees every minute they're on the premises. With CCTV cameras and proximity cards, employers know when each employee goes to and returns from lunch or breaks. The employer can document how long an employee remains in the toilet, making it difficult for those who read the entire morning paper on the pot. One New York hotel encountered a lawsuit when its security officers installed surveillance CCTV cameras in employees' toilets.

Private companies spend a lot of time and effort spying on employees. Some scrutiny is understandable. When you see a battery of ceiling domes containing closed-circuit cameras spaced over check-out lines, you can be sure that this is to combat employee theft. However, other kinds of surveillance, such as cameras in toilets, are not.

Some court decisions have upheld the right of employers to spy on employees. The Puerto Rico Telephone Company placed CCTV cameras to monitor an open area containing desks, chairs, and computers. The U.S. Court of Appeals for the First Circuit ruled that employees in open areas have a "decreased expectation of privacy."[7]

Another pernicious factor is the current practice of down-sizing, sometimes undertaken to get more work out of fewer employees, and at other times the result of exporting jobs to other countries. Layoffs undermine morale, but the typical management response is to blame the victim, the fired or about-to-be-fired employee. The company will hire more guards, install more cameras, and tighten access to the workplace.

The surveillance isn't limited to employees and their physical locations. Employers also want a voyeuristic look into the minds and hearts of those they're considering for employment. Several dozen entrepreneurs provide "integrity tests" purported to show whether an applicant is honest, has a propensity for alcohol or drug abuse, and submits to supervision. These tests are loaded with trick questions, and are

## Chapter Two
## *Private and Public Surveillance*

verbal minefields in which the wrong answers can doom your chances of acceptance.

This intellectual voyeurism is part of the employment picture today, and it's often difficult to find employment without running the gauntlet of "pre-employment screening." You can't avoid it. Of course, you can always refuse to take such a test, but the employer can refuse to consider you for employment.

Workplace violence has also produced a plethora of pop-psych in an effort to cope with the problem. Although many of the statistics that make up the workplace violence picture pertain to armed robberies and other customer assaults, the focus has been on employees. From this, the fear industry has built up a "profile" of the typical violent employee: male, over 40, owns firearms, reads *Soldier of Fortune* magazine, loner, frustrated by problems at work, few relationships away from work, and politically conservative. Unfortunately, this "profile" fits millions of honest, hard-working, non-violent employees, and unnecessarily stigmatizes them. If you're one of these, especially if your name is on a "down-sizing" list, don't be surprised if supervisors watch you with suspicion.

Part of the effort is directed at former employees, on the basis that some may return to attack former supervisors and other employees. One company that tightened its surveillance is Kaiser Permanente, the health maintenance organization. One previously fired woman came back in an angry mood because of her dismissal. Its mid-Atlantic Regional Office now has 16 CCTV cameras, as well as other security measures.[8]

Another aspect of surveillance is careful reading and collation of letters received. Companies often receive angry letters from customers and even former employees, and while the overwhelming majority of these are from law-abiding people, a tiny number presage violence. The letter may not express a threat overtly, but indicates that the writer is mentally disturbed. In such a case, the police can't do anything, and the company is left to its own resources. This is why corporate security officials build up files of letters, trying to correlate the anonymous ones with their writers, in an effort to head off violence.[9]

Probably the most expensive form of surveillance, and the most misunderstood, is the undercover agent. This is a private detective infiltrated into the workplace to ferret out information about employees. The problem may be employee theft, which is legal to investigate, or it may be union activity, which is not. Still, some companies have done this, as well as relied on company spies, employees who report their colleagues' activities to the boss.

When a problem arises, the security director hires an outside investigative agency and chooses a carefully selected person to pose as a new hire. One way or another, a vacancy is created in the suspected department to justify hiring someone new. The undercover agent must be able to do the work, and must have good inter-personal skills. His job is to blend in with the crowd, become accepted, and report back on what he sees and hears.

Simply reporting back often isn't enough. The agent must gain the confidence of other employees, which may involve socializing with them. In some cases, he'll have to participate in illegal activity to gain credibility with his fellow employees.[10]

Of course, this is the theory. In practice, an undercover agent can often entrap another employee. His continued career depends on production; that is, finding suitable targets. A record of failure doesn't guarantee his continued employment with the investigative agency. This then boils down to ethics, and how far he is prepared to go to make himself look good to his employer.

The weakness of many undercover investigations is that they end up as one person's word against another. If the undercover agent suggests to another employee that he steal something, this is entrapment, but unless he's stupid enough to make this suggestion in front of witnesses, it's his word against the employee's. An employee caught with company property in the trunk of his car is in a weak position to claim entrapment.

As we've seen, the bottom line is that, with the official police, you're innocent until proven guilty. With private security agents, everyone is a potential threat or suspect, and you're guilty until proven innocent. As we'll see, private companies spend a lot of effort exchanging data. Once you're on their books, or discs, the stigmatizing information can go literally anywhere.

## Driver's Licenses

Most European countries take great care to document their citizens' lives, beginning with a national identity card. This Single Universal Identifier (SUI) is basic, and citizens carry them at all times, to present when asked by police and other officials. Some countries, such as France and Switzerland, require notifying the police of any change of address.

Although the American people have resisted the introduction of an SUI, in many cases the driver's license serves the same purpose. Most American adults drive, and many who do not have "non-driver's driver's licenses" for identification purposes when cashing checks. The result is that almost everyone over age 16 is documented in this country. As in European countries, holders of licenses must notify the authorities of every address change. The agency is the state motor vehicle bureau, not the police, but driver's licenses are entered into computerized databases, and are accessible by police 24 hours a day.

Today, police expect anyone they confront to show "I.D." Although you're not required to show a driver's license if you're not driving a motor vehicle, failure to do so when a police officer asks you is automatically cause for suspicion.

It's difficult, if not impossible, to forge the driver's licenses of most states. A lot of effort has gone into developing technology to make driver's licenses hard to fake. Not only does the license have the owner's photo, but the document is encapsulated in plastic and many have security features to prevent forgery. The state stamp may be printed across the photo or the signature, and the outer layer has a "retro-reflective" stamp. This is something like a water-mark, impressed into the plastic to be visible when viewed from an angle.

## Public Events and Exhibits

Formerly, attending a public event was very casual. A baseball game might have had a police officer to direct traffic, and even a first-class museum such as New York's Metropolitan had only one armed guard at each entrance. Today, if you visit a historical exhibit such as colonial Williamsburg, Virginia, you'll be under constant surveillance. This 174-acre site has over 200 buildings, and "armed, sworn, uniformed, and plainclothes officers." The site has more than 35 CCTV cameras.[11]

The 1996 Atlanta Olympic Games were promoted as having exemplary security two years before the events. The Department of Defense's little-known Office of Special Events Management was part of the picture. The security covered "airports, Olympic Villages, stadiums, training facilities, and hotels." Electronic means, such as metal detectors, CCTV, and alarm systems were part of the security measures. At times, the security measures must have seemed tiresome, because among the requirements were that all of the 100,000 participants, including athletes, sponsors, volunteers, coaches, etc., had to fill out questionnaires for screening. Those who passed received coded badges, which were checked by guards at every entrance. One hundred and fifty CCTV cameras, and their monitoring equipment, were in place at the various sites.[12]

Despite all this, an unknown person planted a bomb that killed one person and injured many others. The bungled FBI investigation that followed falsely accused one of the Games' security guards at first, but did not produce solid evidence against any suspect. The only certainty is that lawsuits followed the botched investigation.

CCTV is a permanent feature at the Atlanta Zoo, where guards monitor ten cameras, located at the administration building, the vault room, various exhibits, the admissions booth, and elsewhere. Another dozen cameras are in the works. Security is a high priority at this zoo, which has its own security building.[13]

If you shop at a warehouse retailer, such as PACE or Costco, you're familiar with the congested single entrance and exit, and the heavy-handed surveillance employed. Not only do you have to hand over a membership card at check-out, but as you leave, a suspicious security guard double-checks your purchases against your receipt, imposing another delay.[14]

The Superdome, in New Orleans, also uses CCTV to monitor entries and critical sites. These are linked to a control center, where guards monitor them live, instead of relying merely on alarms.[15]

If you have occasion to visit any business, organization, or site where the owners or managers are afraid of an act of aggression, or simply paranoid about security, you're sure to be on someone's CCTV camera and probably recorder as well. If you have occasion to visit a clinic where abortions are performed, for example, you'll be under the lens of a camera as you come up the walk. These cameras work 24 hours a day, and in at least one instance captured on tape a man who pushed a shopping cart laden with an incendiary device through its front door.

## Casinos

Casinos bring in money, often more money than a bank of similar floor area. This makes them attractive targets for confidence artists, robbers, pickpockets, and professional gamblers who have a system for cheating the house. The huge amounts of money involved provide temptations for employees, as well, and the common practice is to put in a comprehensive security system.

The Foxwoods Casino & Resort has 500 guards to oversee 10,000 employees and 30,000 visitors per day. In its security command center, guards monitor over 350 CCTV cameras spotted throughout the premises. VCRs record all views, including the dates and times to enhance evidentiary value. The surveillance command center monitors over an additional 850 CCTV cameras located to monitor gaming operations. These cameras have special macro lenses designed for game surveillance that allow guards to zoom in to view the actions of both dealers and players. Surveillance doesn't stop here. Guards also inspect guests' purses and luggage for "prohibited items that could be used to tamper with gaming devices."[16]

The net result is that if you're present in one of these locales, you're under almost constant surveillance. They're watching you, and if you decide to smoke a joint at a rock concert, an unseen lens will soon be zooming in on you, guiding guards who will come to arrest you. No matter how law-abiding you may be or how innocent your intent, they still watch you. If you resemble the photo of a suspected terrorist, a lens will pinpoint you, and soon suspicious guards will surround you to check you out.

Despite this technological vigilance, the system doesn't work very well. Women's health care clinics all have CCTV cameras, many have armed guards, and still suffer attacks. The security in place was unable to prevent a sophisticated multiple bombing in Atlanta, Georgia, in 1996. The bomber placed a bomb at the clinic, but this was a "sucker bomb," a device to attract attention and draw police officers to the scene.[17] After they'd arrived, a more powerful bomb went off, for the purpose of killing or injuring police and bomb disposal personnel.

## Starting Them Off Young

Perhaps the most pernicious feature of the fear industry and its accomplices is conditioning children to accept constant surveillance as a normal part of life. Using the carrying of weapons into school by a few students as a pretext, schools have begun to allow their corridors to be covered by CCTV cameras. Entrances have metal detectors and x-ray machines.[18]

Some schools require all students, faculty, and other staff to wear picture I.D. at all times while on school grounds. This introduces children to the prospect of carrying I.D. badges the rest of their lives. The reason given, of course, is "protecting students."[19]

Unfortunately, there's a real concern that students and faculty under the eyes of constantly monitored cameras might find the atmosphere oppressive. This is why one school principal has his cameras record, but nobody constantly watching the screens.[20]

To date, none of the schools surveyed have installed CCTV in areas where people normally expect privacy, such as toilets and locker rooms. Some schools use dummy cameras as deterrents, although this could create liability if a student is attacked under the blind eye of a dummy camera.[21]

Inanimate objects such as cameras are not the only dangers students face. Occasionally, school personnel put pressure on children to become informers at an early age. Some teachers, when they can't find out who shot a spitball or committed other misconduct, announce that everyone in the class will go to detention unless someone comes forward to identify the perpetrator.

All of this is for the purpose of "protecting children," an emotionally appealing reason. It's heavy-handed because in practice, children have fewer rights than adults, and often don't know when their rights are being violated for their "protection." Guards who suspect that a child may be carrying contraband can order the child to turn out his pockets, and in some cases there have even been strip searches.

There have been several ridiculous examples of children being apprehended and suspended from school on the pretext of carrying guns or drugs. One "gun" was a model pistol an inch long. One girl was suspended for having an over-the-counter painkiller in her purse.

The surveillance continues well into a student's educational career, and even becomes more sophisticated. Duke University security guards use a special card to keep track of students' movements and transactions. This is the "Duke Card," a combination I.D., debit, and access card that every student, faculty member, and university employee carries.

This program began in 1985, with a photo-I.D. card that had a magnetic stripe on its back. This was not only for identification, but to enable students to open debit accounts and pay for purchases at university cafeterias and university stores. At one stroke, the guard force had access to cardholders' financial transactions, and it was not much of an exaggeration to say that they knew what each student had eaten for breakfast.

The university guard force procured upgraded cards in 1990, and the new cards, combined with access control devices, controlled entry into parking lots, recreational facilities, student residences, and other school buildings. Today, it's literally true that Duke University guards can pinpoint where everyone is every moment while they are on campus.

The new card system is very comprehensive, and the university also uses it to control access to vending machines and athletic events. There are about a quarter-million Duke Card transactions by the 20,000 cardholders every day, all of which are stored in the computer. This is a permanent record, because year-old computer records go onto tapes for archiving.[22]

University guards found the comprehensive tracking and record-keeping useful for them when one day someone placed a dummy fire-bomb made with a Gatorade bottle in the university registrar's office. The guards obtained a list of every Duke Card holder who had recently entered the building where the fire-bomb was found, and another list of every cardholder who had purchased Gatorade at the campus store. Only one name was on both lists. They questioned him and he "confessed." Based on his confession, he went to prison.

This case is disturbing for several reasons. First is that campus police ignored the possibility that the Gatorade bottle could easily have been bought at another store. They also ignored the possibility that it could have been bought by a person other than the perpetrator, and fished out of the trash by the perpetrator. There is also the intense pressure that hardened police can bring to bear on a young, impressionable, and suggestible mind in order to coerce a confession.

There is ample evidence that police can pressure a confession from an innocent person. Cops do not hesitate to use various psychological tricks to make their captive feel that evidence of his guilt is beyond doubt. One way is to tell him falsely that his fingerprints were found at the scene. Another is to tell him that a witness identified him. Yet another lie they use is to show the captive a file folder, telling him that evidence of his guilt is in the folder.[23]

Why would a person who knows he's innocent decide to admit falsely that he was guilty, instead of continuing to try to convince interrogators of his innocence? One reason is emotional fatigue after hours of answering questions. Another, and possibly more compelling, is the promise of a "deal," a lighter charge and penalty in return for a confession. If the interrogators succeed in convincing their prisoner that the evidence against him is overwhelming, and he has no hope of defeating the charge, they can persuade him to lie to obtain a lesser penalty.

High-tech I.D. cards appear to be in almost everybody's future. A small employer can turn them out on his desktop computer, according to advertisements in *Security Management*. Identatronics, Inc., of 425 Lively Blvd., Elk Grove Village, IL 60007, features a "Video Supercard" with the card-holder's color photo, a bar code, magnetic strips, holograms, and other high-security features. Turning out one of these requires a PC equipped with Windows 3.1, and an Identatronics Video Supercard System.[24]

Another company providing similar equipment is:

Imagis Cascade
1027 Pandora Avenue
Victoria, British Columbia
Canada, V8V 3P6
Phone: (250) 383-4201
Fax: (250) 383-4705
Web site: http://www.imagis-cascade.com

Imagis promises full-color identification cards from the user's desktop computer.

## The Surveillance Society

They're watching you, but it's even worse in some other countries, even those we consider solidly democratic and Western. Let's take a look at what's happening in Great Britain, one of our NATO allies, where public surveillance is well on its way to becoming total.

Although British public CCTV surveillance began as a private effort in 1975, with merchants setting up cameras covertly for fear of public disapproval, the government soon stepped in, while some wondered if this was the beginning of a new Orwellian era.

Today, about 120 British municipalities use CCTV to oversee public areas, such as streets, parks, shopping centers, parking lots, and underground walkways. During the 1980s large-scale crime, such as riots, strikes, and other public disorders softened up public opinion enough to allow the government to expand surveillance. IRA terrorism contributed to the panic, and the government proceeded to set up what some call "The Surveillance Society."[25]

The next step will be to install software to recognize faces. Software & Systems International, of Slough, England, developed a system called "Mandrake," which scans CCTV images and picks out any face in its memory. With a library of wanted faces, it provides an alert if it recognizes any similar face on a CCTV screen.[26]

The atmosphere of constant scrutiny is becoming oppressive in Holland, where the Dutch government seems "obsessed" with setting up electronic surveillance of its citizens. Cameras are in train stations, airports, public streets, on top of bridges, and even in private places, such as stores, bars, buses, and taxis. Holland saw its first attack against Photo-Radar, when a driver jumped out of his vehicle to place a piece of tape over the lens.[27]

This is the same mechanism at work that we see in the United States. The media and the government exaggerate and play up a threat, using it to justify further surveillance and restrictions on freedom. In the United States, the city of Baltimore has launched a pilot public surveillance program. The cities of Virginia Beach, Virginia, and Tacoma, Washington, have CCTV already covering the streets.

Of course, proponents of the surveillance society are very enthusiastic about the program. Two British police officers gleefully described an instance (Who knows where? They didn't name the city) in which a mugger practiced his craft in front of a CCTV camera, and was immediately arrested by police. They claim that the British public now "welcomes" surveillance.[28]

## It Can't Happen Here?

While the "surveillance society" appears to be more active and oppressive overseas, we're seeing its practical introduction here, as well. Playing upon public fear of crime, the city of Phoenix, Arizona, is conducting a pilot project to place a surveillance camera on one public bus. The plan is to procure new buses already wired for surveillance cameras. In Tucson, 19 buses already have cameras, with another 25 coming by the end of 1997. The Tempe Elementary School District has been operating cameras on buses since 1995.[29]

Thus we see that overt and covert surveillance are not only with us, they seem to be here to stay. Despite the misgivings of many ordinary citizens, enough remain convinced that they're being watched for their own good, and they tolerate it.

## Notes:

1. Slahor, Dr. Stephanie, "Partners in Crimefighting: Police and Private Security," *Access Control*, July, 1997, p. 31.
2. Sollars, Robert D., "The Taming of The Workplace," *Security Management*, March, 1996, p. 41.
3. Halloran, Liz, "Stealing on the Job: A Guilt-Free World?" *Albuquerque Journal*, August 18, 1997, Business Outlook, p. 23.
4. Personal experiences of the author.
5. Halloran, Liz, "Stealing on the Job: A Guilt-Free World?" *Albuquerque Journal*, August 18, 1997, Business Outlook, p. 23.
6. "Top Security Threats For The 21st Century: What Every Security Professional Should Know," Pinkerton Service Corporation, 1997.
7. Anderson, Teresa, "Legal Reporter," *Security Management*, July, 1997, p. 127.

8. Nieman, Ron, and Ransom, Jonathan, "Healthy Security For an HMO," *Security Management*, August, 1995, pp. 91-96.
9. Post, Jerrold M., "More Than A Figure of Speech," *Security Management*, December, 1996, pp. 38-44.
10. O'Connell, E. Paul, "Is A Ruse The Best Route?" *Security Management*, December, 1995, pp. 26-30.
11. McDaniel, Danny, "Safeguarding Virginia's Colonial Past," *Security Management*, July, 1994, pp. 6A-12A.
12. Keener, James, "Integrating Security Into The Atlanta Games," *Security Management*, July, 1994, pp. 14A-15A.
13. Burgess, Cary S., "Security and the Beast," *Security Management*, September, 1997, pp. 56-61.
14. Bridges, Curtis, "A Pound of Prevention For A Ton of Merchandise," *Security Management*, July, 1994, pp. 22A-23A.
15. Anderson, Teresa, "Security Sports A Winning Strategy," *Security Management*, July, 1994, pp. 24A-26A.
16. Azano, Harry J., "Making Security A Sure Bet," *Security Management*, November, 1994, pp. 43-44.
17. Soukhanov, Anne H., "Word Watch," *Atlantic Monthly*, August, 1997, p. 100.
18. Murphy, Joan R., "Reading, Writing, and Intervention," *Security Management*, August, 1992, p. 26.
19. Gips, Michael A., "Securing the Schoolyard," *Security Management*, March, 1996, p. 48.
20. *Ibid.*, p. 49.
21. *Ibid.*, p. 53.

22. Kirch, John F., "Drawing The Right Card," *Security Management*, September, 1997, pp. 62-70.
23. Rommel, Bart, *Dirty Tricks Cops Use*, Port Townsend, Washington, Loompanics Unlimited, 1993, pp. 75-107.
24. Advertisement, *Security Management*, September, 1997, p. 67.
25. Poole, Robert, and Williams, Derek, "Success in the Surveillance Society," *Security Management*, May, 1996, pp. 29-33.
26. Law & Order, *International News*, "Camera Picks Out Faces," August, 1997, p. 6.
27. Kole, William J., "Dutch Uneasy Under Gaze of Ubiquitous Spy Cameras," Associated Press, *Albuquerque Journal*, August 10, 1997, p. A13.
28. Poole, Robert, and Williams, Derek, "Success in the Surveillance Society," *Security Management*, May, 1996, p. 29.
29. "Cameras To Keep Eye On Phoenix Bus Riders," *Gun Week*, Sept. 10, 1997, p. 12.

# Chapter Three
# Surveillance as Intimidation

One very important purpose of surveillance is intimidation, and this can become very frightening to ordinary people. By contrast, we'll see that surveillance is not intimidating at all to some very dangerous people.

## Retail Surveillance

Retail surveillance is big business because retailing itself is big business. Retail income for 1995 was roughly $1.4 trillion. Reported losses, from accidents, employee pilferage, and shoplifting, reached about $27 billion.[1] This is why, when you enter a store, they're watching you.

By now, we're all used to seeing shiny or black domes in retail store ceilings, and we all know that they contain hidden cameras. It doesn't take much imagination to understand that the cameras are hidden so that potential shoplifters and armed robbers can't tell if a particular camera is pointing at them.

Some businesses install these black plastic domes for intimidation only. One convenience store has two security mirrors and a black plastic dome installed above the counter to suggest that those within range were under videotape surveillance.[2]

**Figure One**
*This sinister black dome contains a CCTV camera with a revolving mount and a zoom lens. Actually, it might even be a dummy, placed in the ceiling for intimidation. You can't tell by looking at it.*

There's some evidence that CCTV doesn't intimidate or deter armed robbers, though. A 1995 survey among convicted armed store robbers in prison presented a picture very different from what many retailers and their guards believe. The first priority for armed robbers is escape, which is why they often hit small stores with the exit near the cash register. The amount of money available was a secondary factor, although many

*Chapter Three*
*Surveillance as Intimidation*

robbers were aware that convenience stores keep less cash on hand than in recent years. Most did not regard CCTV as a deterrent. One finding which should surprise nobody was that robbers did not consider unarmed security guards as threats or deterrents.[3]

**Figure Two**
*This lighter-colored ceiling dome is lower-profile, and probably contains a real camera. The idea is to watch both customers and employees who might slip something into their pockets while stocking shelves.*

CCTV makes later apprehension and conviction of robbers easier, but many robbers don't take this into account, knowing that escaping the scene is the main consideration. A small store that has the cash register near the exit fits the bill perfectly, which is an important reason that convenience stores are often known as "Stop and Robs."

One case that ended up in court illustrates the failure of deterrence. A customer in a convenience store was stabbed by another customer, and he sued the store for negligence, alleging that the store's security was inadequate. The U.S. Tenth Circuit Court of Appeals decided that he didn't have a case.[4]

Many surveillance cameras in retail stores are installed but not manned. In many outlets, only those above the cash registers are overseen by security personnel, because the cash register area is critical. Experience has shown that retailers, like other sorts of businesses, lose more from employee theft than pilfering by outsiders. About 50 to 70 percent of losses result from internal theft.[5] Dishonest check-out clerks short-change customers, allow accomplices to pass through without checking all of the merchandise, and take money from the registers in various innovative and creative ways. These include voiding out sales and false refunds.[6]

Most, about 70 percent, of employees would never steal from their employers, while about 20 percent will if given the opportunity. A minority, the remaining 10 percent, are dedicated thieves, and will try to steal from employers and fellow workers alike.[7]

Although only ten percent of employees are hard-core thieves, the fear industry's answer is to survey them all. They do this with cameras, audio equipment, and other electronic devices.

The camera domes in the rest of the store are mainly there for show. Their cameras may not be under human

*Chapter Three*
*Surveillance as Intimidation*

scrutiny, or may be turned off. Some stores employ plainclothes security guards who monitor the cameras part-time, trying to spot shoplifters. In some cases, the domes are empty. It's impossible to tell by casual scrutiny, because the domes are either black or have a reflective surface to prevent you from seeing the camera inside.

Retail surveillance cameras are often hooked up to videotape recorders by coaxial or fiber optic cable. The value of a VCR is that it provides evidence to be used in a prosecution. Without a video recording, it would be the security officer's word against that of the shoplifter. A tape often prompts an immediate confession and a guilty plea.

Not all surveillance cameras are behind domes. Some are truly covert, as is the surveillance set up by the Long John Silver's fast food chain. When management suspected certain groups of employees of working together to divert cash, they installed covert cameras. The effort was successful, and the company fired and prosecuted the employees. It didn't stop there, however, as the company decided to equip all stores with CCTV.[8]

However, some retailers go a step further, using equipment that provides video, audio, and cash register transactions on a single tape. The purpose is not only to combat employee theft, but to let employees know that they're being watched. The technique is to observe positive incidents as well as negative ones, and to make sure cashiers receive compliments regarding their positive job performance. This reinforces the knowledge that they're under observation.[9]

This heavy-handedness comes under the category of "Friendly Fascism," the electronic equivalent of mink-lined handcuffs. To a security director, any means is justifiable as long as he can get away with it.

Not surprisingly, the demand for covert surveillance cameras is increasing. The September, 1997, issue of *Security Management*, official publication of the American Society for Industrial Security, has an advertisement by a company billing itself "The Leader in Covert Video Systems." TR Manufacturing, Spring Valley, NY, advises readers; "Don't Gamble on Your Covert Video System: Place The Sure Bet!"[10]

## Shopping Malls

Shopping malls, especially newer ones, are often festooned with CCTV cameras. Sawgrass Mill Mall, in Sunrise, Florida, opened in 1990, with more than 90 cameras throughout the mall. Cameras are in plain view, "to provide a deterrent."[11] Even the dumpsters are under surveillance, to prevent non-mall personnel from using them. For more serious purposes common areas are under the lenses, to help guards cope with crimes such as purse-snatching.

## Women's Health Care Clinics

Practically all of the shrinking number of clinics where abortions are performed in the United States have CCTV systems, to survey and record events inside and outside the clinic. Ostensibly, this is a counter-measure against violence, but in fact it's a convenient way to record the faces of peaceful protesters as well. If you're part of an anti-abortion protest, you'll end up on tape, no matter how peaceful and law-abiding your demonstration may be.

Another point is that every person approaching or entering a clinic, where abortions are performed, for whatever purpose, is on tape. A woman coming to a clinic to have her baby aborted may not be thinking of this, but her presence becomes part of a permanent record, and available to clinic officials and law enforcement officers who have a court order.

## Banks

Banks are noted for surveillance cameras, and these are active. Each camera's output is recorded. This is standard bank security practice, for three reasons. Security cameras provide deterrence, evidence for prosecution, and aid in identifying bank robbers. At least, that's the theory.

Their effectiveness is questionable. We have had an upsurge in bank robberies in recent years, mainly because amateurs have discovered that bank robbery is lucrative, but remarkably few of these result in identifiable photos of the perpetrators, for obvious reasons. A hat, false mustache, and sunglasses serve to hide the features and make positive identification of the perpetrator impossible, and bank robbers know this.

Los Angeles, California, identified as the "bank robbery capital of the world" in a September 11, 1997 broadcast of *48 Hours*, has many security features in its banks, including CCTV cameras. The FBI agent interviewed explained how amateurish and inept many bank robbers are, but was unable to explain why so few were apprehended in southern California. Those apprehended were either very unlucky or they robbed too many banks in a short period of time, thus taking too many risks.

Experience shows that banks employing armed guards suffer fewer robberies than those relying on security cameras alone. The only true deterrent is the risk of being shot dead, and only the most hardened robbers, or the most foolhardy, will face an armed guard when a much safer alternative is just down the street.

Some banks have gone even further in heavy-handed security measures. Banks in Puerto Rico and the United States have put in closed entrances similar to airlocks to control customer access. The Mellon Bank, spread over Pennsylvania, Delaware, and Maryland, introduced enclosed metal detection gates to spot anyone trying to bring a firearm into a bank. Cubicles made of bullet-resistant glass enclosed metal detector portals. An interlocking system required that anyone entering wait for the outer door to close and lock before pushing open the inner door. Floor sensors prevented more than one person from entering a cubicle at one time.[12]

There were reports that customer "acceptance" of this procedure was very high. This isn't surprising. After several decades of being herded like sheep at airports, people have become conditioned to the inevitability of enhanced and more oppressive "security," and submit to more encroachments on their personal liberty.

## Employee Surveillance

In other contexts, surveillance cameras serve similar purposes. In a factory or office, the presence of cameras shows employees that someone's always peering over their shoulders and that everything they do may be documented. Taking long coffee breaks, slipping a tool into the pocket, and chatting with other employees are done under the camera's all-seeing eye. Some managers are aware that theft of time, such as falsifying time cards and sleeping on the job, is costly.[13] Pervasive CCTV coverage is security's answer. Presumably, this makes employees paranoid about being watched, and fearful of breaking company rules.

## Countering Union Activities

Employers prefer to be sovereign in their own businesses, and resent union organizing and collective bargaining. The history of labor-management relations in this country is filled with incidents of acrimony, strikes, lock-outs, and even violence. The National Labor Relations Act and its amendments legislate proper conduct in labor disputes, but many employers see union activity as mainly a security problem.

This is why companies with unions charge their security departments with the task of surveillance of union activities. While it's illegal to spy on employees with regard to union activities, the techniques themselves are neutral and subject to ambiguous interpretation.

An article in *Security Management* outlines what employers can legally do to resist unionization, and explains tactics used to delay union recognition. The article lists tell-tale signs of union organization activity, such as employees shunning a supervisor with whom they normally speak, taking longer breaks, and groups lapsing into silence at the approach of a supervisor.[14]

What is "legal" and what is not often depends on what you can prove in court. Surveillance cameras installed ostensibly for security can also serve to record employees' meetings. In companies where a CCTV system is already in place, it will be very hard for a union to prove that the cameras are for the purpose of spying on union activities.

When strikes occur, company guards naturally are charged with protecting company property. However, there are security agencies specializing in anti-union surveillance. These perform surveillance of picket lines, ostensibly to guard against violence or other illegal activities on the part of the strikers, but also to photograph who is on the line, for intimidation. It doesn't take much imagination to understand that, after the strike ends, management can review the films and tapes and single out strikers or union leaders for reprisals.

Several security companies specialize in labor strikes. One that calls itself the "Asset Protection Team" features a uniformed cameraman in its advertisement, with the title "Gotcha!" Adding to the intimidation is the baton hanging from the guard's belt and a heavy flashlight, the sort that can cause a serious injury, on his left hip.[15]

Even more threatening is the image presented by the Special Response Corporation. Promising to provide one to 200 "specially trained and equipped professionals," this company has an intimidating photo of a helmeted trooper equipped with a shield in its advertisement.[16]

The nature and tone of "security" measures are certainly to intimidate both employees and the public. The picture of the all-seeing eye, once a myth, is today reality. It can only become worse, as the heavy hand of ubiquitous surveillance reaches further and further.

## Notes:

1. Hayes, Read R., "Selling The Concept of Loss Prevention," *Security Management*, December, 1996, p. 53.
2. Anderson, Teresa, "Legal Reporter, Premises Liability," *Security Management*, October, 1997, p. 88.
3. Erickson, Rosemary J., and Stethson, Arnie, CPP, "Crimes of Convenience," *Security Management*, October, 1996, pp. 60-63.
4. Anderson, Teresa, "Legal Reporter, Premises Liability," *Security Management*, October, 1997, p. 88.
5. Benny, Daniel J., "Reducing The Threat Of Internal Theft," *Security Management,* July, 1992, p. 40.

6. Tesorero, Francis X., Jr., "Tune in To Turn Off Employee Theft," *Security Management*, February, 1993, p. 34.
7. Benny, Daniel J., "Reducing The Threat Of Internal Theft," *Security Management*, July, 1992, p. 40.
8. Price, William, "Reeling In Dishonest Employees," *Security Management*, August, 1995, pp. 48-52.
9. Tesorero, Francis X., Jr., "Tune in To Turn Off Employee Theft," *Security Management*, February, 1993, p. 34.
10. Advertisement, *Security Management*, September, 1997, p. 32.
11. Perry, Mary E. B., "Safe Shopping at The Mall," *Security Management*, June, 1992, pp. 47-48.
12. Foyle, Michael P., "Closing The Door To Easy Money," *Security Management*, January, 1995, pp. 61-64.
13. Benny, Daniel J., "Reducing The Threat Of Internal Theft," *Security Management*, July, 1992, p. 40.
14. Plifka, John W., "The Right to Resist The Union Label," *Security Management*, June, 1993, pp. 61-66.
15. Advertisement, *Security Management*, May, 1997, p. 75.
16. *Security Management*, February, 1994, p. 58.

# Chapter Four
# Digging Up Dirt

One purpose of surveillance is to dig up dirt on rivals, potential blackmail victims, and adversaries of commercial clients. Private eyes snoop to get the goods on their clients' enemies, and if successful, can deliver dirt that the client can use to influence them.

Of course, governments do this too. One magnificent example, if it actually occurred as reported, was the electronic espionage undertaken during the fall of 1993 against President Clinton's guests at the Asia-Pacific Economic Cooperation (APEC) Summit Meeting. A multi-agency effort involving the FBI, U.S. Secret Service, and the National Security Agency, among others, disclosed evidence of serious misconduct by some delegates.[1]

The various agencies concerned gave "no comment" replies to questions. The nature of the allegations is explosive. One series of tapes supposedly showed "underage boys engaging in sexcapades with men in several rooms over a period of days."[2] The reason no criminal prosecution resulted is that it would have allegedly endangered national security. Another seamy aspect is that FBI agents allegedly received kickbacks from manufacturers of the electronic equipment used for the surveillance.

What was this for? Apart from providing material for potential blackmail operations, there was economic intelligence. One tidbit concerned a deal for two Boeing 737 airliners sought by the government of Vietnam. The Clinton administration allegedly facilitated a deal to ingratiate itself with the Vietnamese Government, and to elicit support for the Democratic National Committee (DNC). As has developed since, contributions to the DNC from various Asian persons and interest groups have been a major bone of contention.

Blackmail is, of course, much harder to uncover, because both sides have a compelling interest to see that the real story never sees the light of day. Most of the people bugged were second-rank staffers, not top foreign government leaders, and these make excellent espionage targets. This means that they're less vulnerable to the vagaries of government staffing. Ministers come and go, but administrative assistants can remain in many cases, and continue to serve the people with a hold on them.

It helps a lot to have an administrative assistant in your back pocket. He can provide classified information, influence his boss, plant information you want planted, disregard or "lose" reports, provide information on other government employees vulnerable to suborning, provide introductions to people you wish to meet or influence, and serve as a check on information received from other agents in his government.

*Chapter Four*
*Digging Up Dirt*

The nature of the information obtained through bugging people who attended this summit meeting presents interesting possibilities, because of its very nature. First, many other countries are less tolerant of sex crimes against children than the United States, and have heavier penalties. Secondly, sexual exploiters sometimes form rings to pursue their illicit interests. In the Western World, there are several openly pedophilic and pederastic associations, some on the Internet. In Third World countries pedophiles and pederasts have to be much more discreet, but any such network penetrated by a Western intelligence agency offers the perfect opportunity to milk its members dry.

## Notes:

1. Maier, Timothy W., "Snoops, Sex, and Videotape," *Insight*, September 29, 1977, pp. 7-9.
2. *Ibid.*, p. 8.

# Chapter Five
# Commercial Motives

Some surveillance takes place simply for dollars-and-cents. Chances are that you've seen advertisements by supermarkets for special "discount" cards for their customers. These cards, working with bar codes, are issued upon request to anyone, and the marketers promise special "values," "discounts," and other incentives to card-users. What they really do with them is fascinating.

These cards are used in conjunction with the laser scanners designed to read bar codes on products. The customer presents his card to the checker before starting the transaction. After the checker scans the card, the store's computer gives the advertised discounts.

"Discounts" are disappointing. Typically, they are a few pennies off the posted price. More than one supermarket has, to the dismay of alert customers who don't take everything for granted, jacked up all of its prices to cover these "discounts." The net result is that the customer with a card gets no more of a break than the customer who shops at a competing store that does not use these cards.

These cards are marketing ploys. One of the highest priorities in marketing is compiling target lists. These may be lists of childless couples, couples with small children, single males, people with pets, people with elderly relatives living at home, those with uncommon sexual habits, and others. Sharply focused lists allow great economy in marketing efforts, because they significantly reduce the waste in mailing advertisements to unsuitable people. Tightly focused lists bring top dollar in the shadowy market of customer lists.

Tracking what an individual or family member buys at the supermarket can build up a sharp profile of the type of people involved. Your discount card, and the way it correlates everything you buy to your name, tells a marketing specialist a lot about you.

Do you pay with cash, check, or food stamps? This, too, can provide a guide to your status.

Do you buy diapers regularly? Then obviously you have a small child. The number of diapers you buy also tells the number of small children you have in your household.

On the other hand, if a lot of your expenditures are for prescriptions, this tells the market research specialist that someone in your household has health problems. The nature of the prescription, such as insulin, can pinpoint the illness. If you buy Geritol, Centrum Silver, and other senior-citizen products, this suggests an aging relative in your household.

Are caviar, champagne, brandy, lobster tails, and filet mignon regularly on your shopping list? If so, you've provided important clues to your economic status. On the other hand, if corned beef hash, tomato soup, and

## Chapter Five
## Commercial Motives

ground beef predominate, the marketing specialist has you pegged as someone living marginally.

What proportion of your supermarket ticket is for food? If a lot, it helps estimate how large your family is. If unusually low, it suggests that you live alone and/or eat out a lot.

What sort of food products do you buy? Are they mostly prepared foods, which require minimal preparation? This suggests that the adults in your household don't have time to prepare full-scale meals.

Do you buy kosher products during Passover? If so, you've just documented your religion.

What about other purchases? What can they tell about your life-style that would interest a market research specialist? Do you buy alcoholic beverages? How much, and how often? Does this correlate with averages for the number of people in your household?

Car polish? Of course, you have a car or truck. Pet food? Is it dog food or cat food?

Do you know if you buy more or less than your neighborhood's average in soap and other cleaning products? This tells something about your personal cleanliness, and how clean you keep your home.

If you buy a certain brand of vodka heavily advertised in homosexual magazines, plus condoms and lubricating jelly, you don't have to go any further. They have your number.

The frightening aspect of this is that it's not for demographic or statistical purposes. Each purchase you make is linked to your name and address. They know who and what you are by what you buy.

Supermarket trackers use deception to cover their real motives. They prepare public-relations pablum to feed to customers to make their electronic card efforts appear perfectly innocuous. However, as we'll see in the section on the Internet, server and site operators work hand in hand in tracking your interests. The Internet is ready-made for surveillance without your consent or even knowledge.

## Industrial Espionage

If you work for a living, you may be the target of surveillance without your consent, or even knowledge, because industrial espionage is a growth industry. If your employer has a secret process that is a trade secret, a customer list, or even confidential sales figures, he'll be concerned about protecting his secrets.

If you work in research and development, or in a crucial manufacturing process, your employer may have asked you to sign a "non-disclosure" form before you began your employment. This means that you will not disclose sensitive information (and the boss determines what is sensitive) to any unauthorized person. The agreement may also have had a clause that you would not take up employment with a competitor for a certain time after leaving your present employer. Violation exposes you to civil penalties.

You'll also notice security measures in the workplace. Those cameras and motion sensors aren't because your boss worries about how many minutes you spend in the toilet, but to detect unauthorized visitors during the workday, and intruders after hours. There will be a company security director, responsible for both physical security and personnel reliability. Physical security can easily include checking secure work areas for bugs.

Determining personnel reliability is the more challenging task, and you, the employee, can be the subject of investigation by both your employer and someone seeking to steal his secrets. The security director is interested in personal weaknesses, such as gambling, which can bring a need for quick money. He's also interested in personal lifestyle secrets, which can expose a person to blackmail. The security director will investigate you at intervals, checking out your lifestyle to see if you're living above your means, and this includes driving by your home to see if you've got a Lexus parked in front when your salary is Neon-level.

Similar investigative techniques are in use by the "other side," a business rival who wants information you may be able to provide. Gossip about competitors' personnel is valuable, and his employees may be under instructions to report personal contacts at trade shows, social contacts, and other information. At trade shows, especially, a member of the competitor's security department posing as an accountant or engineer will try to develop information about the other company's staff. A lot can come from after-hours socializing.

If they center on you, they'll be interested in whether you're married to a wife who wants more amenities than your salary can provide, or whether you have medical bills piling up, or whether you have gambling debts. They'll also want to know how you feel about your employer, including if he's treating you fairly and paying you satisfactory wages. Some of this information can come up during a casual conversation over drinks. More information can come from interviewing your friends and neighbors. Still more can come from following you around town for a day or two.

If you visit a hospital, for example, you might be seeing an acquaintance, or you might have a seriously ill relative. If you go off alone, leaving your wife at home, and stop for several hours at another person's residence, this could be a perfectly innocent visit, or a clue to an illicit relationship.

Do you answer "blind ads" (job ads that do not disclose the company) in the classified section to keep abreast of your job market, or because you're looking for something else? If so, you may be exposing yourself to discovery and exploitation. A rival who places a blind ad expects to catch a few of his competitor's employees. Under the pretext of interviewing them for employment, the rival tries to winnow a few trade secrets from them. Deft questioning of a naive employee can produce a lot for little effort because, wanting the job, the employee is eager to please.

The blind ad might also come from your employer. If you send your résumé to a postal box number it may end up on the desk of your company's security director, who naturally wants to know of anyone who is thinking of leaving. Your name might then go on a short list for reference during the next down-size.

International industrial espionage has become the number one priority with the end of the Cold War. In this regard, the worst offenders are France and Israel, according to a consensus in the American security industry.

# Chapter Six
# The Myth of "Security"

They're watching you for your own good. At least, that's what they want you to believe. Sometimes, it's true. Most often, it's not for your protection, but for the protection and benefit of the people doing the watching, or their employers. The reason often given, that of "security," is merely pablum for public consumption.

The excuse for surveillance is "security," most prominently and self-righteously expressed in the field of airline travel. In reality, very few airliners are either hijacked or blown up, but there's money in overreaction. The fear industry earns many millions of dollars a year providing the illusion of protection against terrorism.

We see the pecuniary motive clearly in a letter published in the April, 1996, issue of *Security Management* in response to an article that had suggested that the federal government should take over airport security from private companies. The letter's author protests that this view is "detrimental to private security." The author does not argue that private security guards can do a better job than government employees, only that the publication should not present articles that endorse a federal takeover, thereby depriving private security operators of the business.₁

**Figure Three**
*Federal Aviation Administration rules now prohibit the carrying of pepper spray, Mace, and Kubotans, as pictured here, beyond the security checkpoints. Actually, this Kubotan is made of plastic, and if you take off the key ring you can carry it aboard an aircraft in your pocket. Anyway, no airliner has ever been hijacked by a person "armed" with a Kubotan.*

Aiding and abetting the fear industry in frightening the public are the media, using "body-bag journalism" as a way of capturing larger audiences for their advertisers. Every media person knows that bad news sells, and this is particularly true in the TV news segment. Emphasizing violent news to the detriment of other stories has created "a nation of cynical, fearful viewers."₂

This type of sensationalism, preoccupied with tragic and violent events, makes it appear that the nation is literally besieged by terrorists. The real picture is much more modest and much less frightening. Realistically, an average of 25 Americans die each year as a result of

*Chapter Six*
*The Myth of "Security"*

terrorism, and most of these killings take place overseas where Americans work in violence-prone countries. Ordinary, nitty-gritty murders kill between 20 and 25 thousand Americans each year at home, according to FBI figures. Traffic accidents run in the 40,000-per-year range. In plain language, if you're going to die violently this year, the odds are that it will be in a traffic accident. Second place is murder by a relative, friend, or stranger, as during an armed robbery. Your odds of being killed in a terrorist bombing or shooting are about the same as of winning the lottery.

**Figure Four**
*All of these weapons are made of plastic or fiberglass. The dagger disguised as a comb fits into a pocket and is certainly a deadly weapon, completely invisible to metal detectors, as are the other daggers. Top right shows the "Executive Ice Scraper", useful for scraping ice off somebody's throat. Finally, we see two models of the "JU-JO," bottom and right, which contain lengths of parachute cord for garroting the victim.*

Actually, the incidence of terrorism seems to be declining, despite what one security expert calls the "constant drumbeat" from government, the media, and others that terrorism is on an unprecedented rise. This is based on a careful analysis of FBI and CIA data.3 Counting official figures, we see that the intensity, number, and even lethality of terrorist incidents have been on a decline recently.

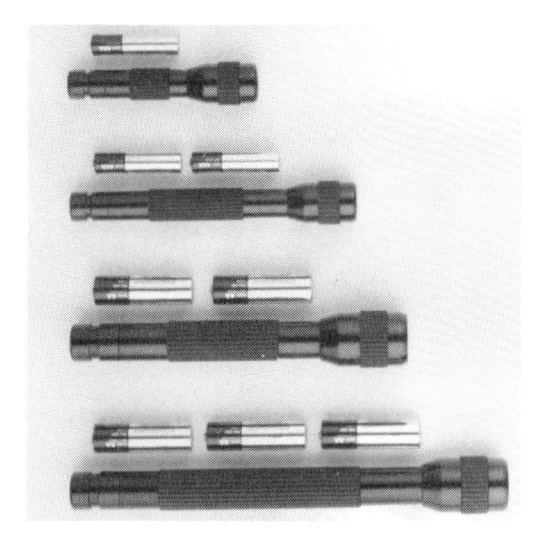

**Figure Five**
*All four of these mini-flashlights are made of metal, perfectly legal, and serve the same purpose as the Kubotan. You can carry one of these on board an airliner on your key-ring, in your pocket, or in a belt scabbard. No problem.*

Even these do not affect Americans as much as one might think after seeing the raw figures. Closer analysis shows that almost 40 percent of terrorist attacks during 1995 were committed by a single organization, the Kurdish Workers Party, against Turks and Turkish interests.[4]

This is not good news to those promoting security services and hardware, any more than the end of the Cold War was good news to the purveyors of military hardware. Their response is simply to deny that terrorism is declining, and to collaborate closely with the media in promoting feature articles about terrorism to keep the public stimulated.

## Ineffective "Security"

At this point, let's draw the line between genuine security and fake security that consists mainly of boondoggling, employing low-grade people who otherwise might be on welfare, or selling worthless security-related products. Genuine security protects small, limited targets. A good example is the World Trade Center, attacked by a terrorist bomb in February, 1993. Today, there are surveillance cameras, vehicle ground loop detectors, bullet-resistant guard booths, and electronic identification technologies to prevent a recurrence.[5]

The Empire State Building was the site of a shooting when a Palestinian opened fire on a crowd on the 86th-floor observation deck on February 23, 1997. There already was security in force, as cameras filmed the gunman as he rode an escalator, but this wasn't enough to prevent the shooting. Nobody knows why the gunman did it, because he blew his brains out without telling.[6]

Now there is more security. Although the odds of another random shooting in the same place by another nutcake are almost non-existent, there are metal detector gates and x-ray machines controlling access to the observation deck.[7]

Courtroom security is another sensitive area. Courts are point targets, and protecting them is possible, at the cost of excessive surveillance and delaying those with legitimate business in the courts. The U.S. Courthouse at New York's Foley Square has 88 CCTV cameras covering every lobby, every entrance, cashiers' windows, and clerks' offices. Eighty more cameras provide surveillance so that judges may see who is trying to gain entrance to their chambers.[8]

The crux is protecting a point target, which is possible, versus protecting an area target, which is impossible. Area targets are the country's airline system, including airports, the electric power grid, water supplies for all of the United States' cities and towns, the postal system, and other vulnerable resources that are too scattered to defend. However, where the media stir up anxiety, the fear industry stands ready to provide "security," however inadequate.

After TWA Flight 800 dropped out of the sky in the summer of 1996, the media helped the fear industry by promoting reports of missiles shot at the airliner by persons unknown. Some fanciful accounts stated the missiles had come from shore, others named a small boat, but all implied that shadowy terrorists had destroyed the aircraft. Further clouding the issue was

*Chapter Six*
*The Myth of "Security"*

that fact that Flight 800 had taken off about a half-hour late, and was on the schedule of a flight headed for Tel Aviv. This brought up the prospect of Arab terrorists, with the memory of the World Trade Center bombing fresh in people's minds. Arab terrorists had, in fact, destroyed an American airliner when they planted a bomb on board Pan American Flight 103 and it detonated over Lockerbie, Scotland, in 1989.

The difficulty of recovering wreckage at the bottom of the sea made it worse, greatly prolonging the investigation, and providing an opportunity for the media to present a year-long tease to their audiences, suggesting without actually stating that there was evidence of terrorist involvement.

The Federal Aviation Administration took advantage of the situation to enhance what it labeled as "security" at the nation's airports. New signs appeared, stating that it was forbidden to bring cans of Mace, pepper spray, or Kubotans past the security checkpoints. This was evidently make-work, as no airliner had ever been hijacked by someone using Mace, pepper spray, or a Kubotan. At the Albuquerque, New Mexico, airport, the new security measure became laughable because the sign was misspelled.

The U.S. Postal Service got into the act, possibly as a reaction to the "Unabomber's" 18-year-long career. During the spring of 1997, signs appeared pasted to mailboxes stating that all parcels weighing more than 16 oz. were to be presented to a clerk inside the post office, and not dropped casually into the mailbox. The alleged reason was to enhance "security." From the start, this new security measure did not work very well.

Perhaps postal executives had doubts about this policy's viability, because it wasn't enforced in all areas.

**Figure Six**
*This mailbox has a sign at the bottom prohibiting deposit of packages weighing over 16 oz. Any competent terrorist, or even a kid with a chemistry set, could make a bomb lighter than that. Toxic chemicals and biological agents can easily fit into packages weighing less than 16 oz.*

Security experts know that letter bombs may weigh less than 16 oz. In fact, about three oz. of Semtex or other high explosive are enough to maim or kill anyone opening the envelope. Likewise for chemical or biological agents. It takes far less than 16 oz. of lethal

*Chapter Six*
*The Myth of "Security"*

virus or chemical poison to kill the occupants of an auditorium.

Possibly postal clerks realized this from the start, as there were several reported instances of parcels heavier than 16 oz. casually dropped into mailboxes and reaching their destinations without delay. Other excessively heavy parcels were returned to the sender. In any event, it was very unclear what postal employees were to do if faced with a parcel heavier than the allowed weight dropped casually into a mailbox. Call the bomb squad? Take it into the post office until a postal inspector arrived to determine the contents of the package? Return it to the sender?

It was unclear exactly what the new regulation was to accomplish, but there existed more than one gigantic loophole. Anyone, whether former employee, unhappy customer, or merely a psychopath with a grudge against the U.S. Postal Service, would be able to drop a lethal parcel into any mailbox, using a false address and return address, secure in the knowledge that the parcel would end up inside a post office, where it could do a lot of harm to employees, customers, and the physical plant. Bombs can be any size, and there is no physical or scientific reason that a vial of nerve gas or biological agent has to be above a certain size or weight.

The post office provides potential saboteurs with a lot of help by posting collection times on every mailbox, including those outside the post office, where the clerk picks up the mail in a cart and immediately brings it inside. Anyone seeking to have a bomb explode inside a post office merely has to put together a bomb and set the timer for an hour after the pick-up time to ensure that it detonates indoors.

Another loophole exists because it doesn't take a rocket scientist to figure out that an excessively heavy and lethal package using the target's name and address as the return address will be delivered there instead of to the addressee. As a hedge against the stupidity of postal employees, the mailing address is totally fictitious, forcing the post office to return the package to the "sender." An extra guarantee is simply not to put any stamps on the package.

The FBI is expanding its anti-terrorist activities. Director Louis Freeh told the Senate Appropriations Committee that the FBI now spends $243 million per year on counterterrorism and has 2,600 employees assigned to it. Freeh stated that domestic terrorists appear to be a more serious problem than foreign ones.[9]

It seems everybody wants to get into the act. Elvid Martinez, Commissioner of the U.S. Bureau of Reclamation, has responsibility for federal dams. Martinez recently announced his plan to create a post of "Security Director" for the 475 dams and 58 hydroelectric dams in his jurisdiction. This was based on a concern that large dams, such as Hoover and Grand Coulee, were vulnerable. In fact, no sabotage had taken place, although an anonymous caller claimed that a paramilitary group had targeted Hoover Dam.[10]

Another incident was almost laughable, except for its lethal ending. A teen-ager was shot and killed by the FBI after he attempted to extort $15,000 by threatening to blow up the Columbia River's Bonneville Dam in

## Chapter Six
## The Myth of "Security"

1996. The teen was armed, but his "detonator" was a cellular phone.

## False Security Seals

Police and other agents often use special seals to prevent tampering. A special adhesive seal can be on a door, envelope, box, or file cabinet to prevent unauthorized opening. In theory, these seals, which can be anything from tape to wire and lead seals, locks, and other anti-tampering devices, will show evidence of any entry. However, the Vulnerability Assessment Team (VAT) at Los Alamos National Laboratories found that they could defeat every seal they tested, and without using high-tech, James Bond methods. This came as a rude shock to a high government official who visited the laboratory and discovered that the seals he and his agency had been using to protect their secrets were vulnerable. In fact, most could be defeated in minutes, using simple and commonly available tools and materials obtainable in hardware stores, KMarts, and other public sources.[11]

"Defeating" a seal means gaining undetected access, and the team found that they could defeat all sorts of seals, using heat, chemical agents, small drills, and other common tools and materials. The time it took to do this varied from three seconds to two hours, with an average time of four minutes. Trained security officers found that it was hard to determine if a particular seal had been breached without careful examination, and even then an inspection wasn't always conclusive.

The implications are frightening, especially to the average consumer who trusts that supermarket product tampering is impossible today because of "tamper-proof" product seals. In reality, it's not terribly difficult to buy a box of tablets or capsules, unseal the foil and plastic wrapping, substitute noxious agents for the ingredients, reseal the package, and put it back on the supermarket shelf without leaving a trace of tampering. Yet, the fear industry is earning millions of dollars producing such bogus security features, and it's only a matter of time before terrorists and pranksters learn how to defeat them.

## Privatization

The rush towards "privatization" has led to some ridiculous extremes, the consequences of which decision-makers are only beginning to appreciate. Federal police used to protect federal government buildings around the country. However, many have been replaced by private guards.[12]

It's worse in nuclear power station protection. Despite the loudly expressed concerns about foreign and domestic terrorists and the threat they pose to nuclear power generating stations, most of these have only private guards for "protection."

Well, what's wrong with privatization? Plenty. First, the private guards are not selected for competency and fidelity, but for how cheaply they'll work. Offering lower pay and benefits to applicants dictates that mainly lower-grade people will apply. Within the private security industry agency executives know very well that there exist almost no state-mandated standards for private security work, and that often they're forced to hire rejects. These are "wannabes" who failed to gain employment with police agencies but who still want to wear a uniform and carry a gun. Despite misgivings, private guard agency managers will hire cheaply because they know that if they don't, their competitor down the block will, and subsequently walk away with the next contract. It's that simple.

Cost-cutting is the main motive for privatization. After more than a quarter-century, we've seen the effect of "privatizing" the post office in the deterioration in its service. As a nation, we can afford this deterioration because the post office isn't important to us. Increasingly, we have learned to use the telephone, fax, e-mail, and the Internet for rapid communications. The U.S. Postal Service is increasingly marginalized as a deliverer of junk mail.

However, when we begin replacing trained and certified police officers with "rent-a-cops" in key services, we're in trouble. These poorly motivated people are not going to work very hard, even if they have the skills, and most definitely do not. A squad of rent-a-cops protecting a nuclear power station is a deadly farce.

## Notes:

1. Del Pino, Luis J., CPP, "Airport Security," *Security Management*, April, 1996, pp. 6-8.

2. "Body-bag Journalism Fuels Cynicism," Fear, *Law Enforcement News*, May 31, 1997, p. 6.
3. Johnson, Larry C., "The Fall of Terrorism," *Security Management*, April, 1997, pp. 26-32.
4. *Ibid.*, p. 26.
5. Carey, Carol, "Preventing Future Nightmares at the World Trade Center," *Access Control*, July, 1997, p. 34.
6. Whitemire, Tim, "2 Dead, 6 Hurt in Empire State Building Shooting," Associated Press, *Albuquerque Journal*, February 24, 1997, p. A10.
7. Garbera, Don, "Security Strikes Back to Ensure Safety of the Empire State Building," *Access Control*, July, 1997, pp. 21-23.
8. Wickizer, Jim, "Recorder In The Court," *Security Management*, August, 1992, pp. 74-75.
9. "Citing Growing Threat, Freeh Expands FBI Anti-terror Efforts," *Law Enforcement News*, May 31, 1997, p. 6.
10. "Those Dam Terrorists," *Law Enforcement News*, May 31, 1997, p. 9.
11. Johnston, Roger G., "The Real Deal on Seals," *Security Management*, September, 1997, pp. 93-100.
12. Hanson, Gayle M. B., "Private Protection is Secure Industry," *Insight*, September 29, 1997, p. 19.

# Chapter Seven
# Investigations

They're watching you if you are collecting any sort of injury-related insurance. Insurance companies are not only slow to pay, they're naturally suspicious, and treat anyone making a claim as guilty until proven innocent. While there may not be any doubt regarding the nature of your injuries, because of doctor's and hospital's records, insurance claims officers are always suspicious regarding the amount of disability. If you're unable to work because of an injury, you can be certain the insurance company will send an investigator to see if you're mowing the lawn or performing another physical task while supposedly incapacitated. This practice is so common that one freelance investigator, Bill Kizorek, advertises in *Security Management*, a publication aimed at the security industry. His ad shows him posing with a telephoto-equipped camera.[1]

You may notice a van parked across the street from your home. The van has hidden apertures for photographing suspects. Inside will be an investigator equipped with cameras, including camcorders, waiting to see if you walk out under your own power while you're supposed to be confined to a wheelchair.

**They're Watching You!**
The Age of Surveillance

They may be watching you if you're a member of any group or organization they don't like. Examples are animal-rights groups, anti-abortion organizations, and homosexual lobbies. Because a few members of these groups have committed acts which they can call "terrorism," or "vandalism," all members are automatically suspect, and sometimes under surveillance. This is called "preventive surveillance," in the lingo of the trade.[2]

Surveillance can be rigorous and all-encompassing in the effort to gather information, identify the members of the group, and ascertain intelligence about the group's future plans. A security expert finds it necessary to caution his peers to remain within the law: "All intelligence operations must remain lawful and within reasonable bounds. Trickery is acceptable; extorting information is not. Being observant in the groups' offices is acceptable; burglarizing their offices is not."[3]

This admirable ideal goes out of focus when we read his next admonition, that obtaining information is more important than building a case that will stand up in court. A videotape of the company president's assassination is less valuable than preventing it.

From this, we can infer that courtroom evidence must follow certain standards. Obtaining information that will never see the light of day allows certain shortcuts. Agents can follow the movements of "suspected activists." Whatever rights these "activists" have are irrelevant if the surveillance remains hidden. Even a break-in might occur, on the basis that it's not a crime if you're not caught.

Surveillance can employ legal methods of checking on the targeted group's legal activities. Public records reveal whether a member has ever run for political office, for example. Securing copies of the organization's publications and propaganda is another recommended technique. Photographing members at public rallies produces pictures that can be useful in aiding witnesses to identify participants if ever there is a court injunction or an act of violence. Another recommended technique is shadowing the group's leaders to obtain information on what they're planning. Infiltrating a group with undercover agents is yet another technique.[4]

A "mole," sent to infiltrate a group, can obtain material from its files. The rewards for such pilfering can be great, among them mailing lists. If you've ever sent for information about any group or organization that a private firm or security agency or "watchdog organization" considers subversive or otherwise dangerous and worthy of investigation, your name will be on a list. If an undercover agent, public or private, ever gets his hands on that list, your name goes on a master suspect list forever.

Let's note here that we're not discussing what the FBI or other police agency might do. This concerns private investigative agencies using police methods to scrutinize people they don't like. Unlike police, private agencies have no official powers to compel cooperation, and as a result they use stealth and guile much more than police do.

A doubly dangerous technique is obtaining information from what the author calls "watchdog organizations." These are private organizations that target what they consider "extremist" groups, and report on their findings.[5]

The problem is that because they are private, they must produce something, usually periodic reports on what their targeted groups are doing. They depend upon private contributions for support, as they do not receive government budgets. This accounts for reports that are often exaggerated and inflammatory. They have to present frightening information to stimulate their supporters to keep contributing money. As private organizations, they can free-wheel a lot, and shade the facts to make it appear that they're doing a wonderful job of keeping track of very dangerous persons.

Informal and private surveillance is another tactic of intimidation. Knowing that if you join an unpopular organization your name will appear on a list has a chilling effect. This is exactly what the list-compilers want.

## Notes:

1. *Security Management*, April, 1993, p. 72.
2. Mendell, Ronald L., "A Cause For Concern," *Security Management*, December, 1994, p. 44.
3. *Ibid.*, p. 45.
4. *Ibid.*, p. 48.
5. *Ibid.*, p. 48.

# Chapter Eight
# Tools and Techniques

They're watching you, using some of the most advanced and sophisticated technology to keep track of where you go, what you do, and even what you say. Visual and audio surveillance are almost everywhere, and some electronic technology allows the watchers to keep track of your movements without cameras or microphones.

## Visual Surveillance

Closed-circuit TV (CCTV) is the most common electronic visual surveillance technique. At the most basic level, hardware and electronic stores sell small black-and-white cameras and monitors for home security. Total cost is between $200 and $300 for the homeowner who wants to see who is at the front door. More elaborate installations, including color cameras, VCRs, and even remote recording, serve for other applications.

Recording can be in two modes: real-time or time-lapse. Real-time is regular TV, at 30 frames per second, showing full motion. Time-lapse selects only a few frames per time period, perhaps one or two per second, to record. The advantage of time-lapse is that it allows one tape to record for a much longer time than real-time recording.

Video electronics can be very sophisticated indeed, and the latest trend is digital video. This allows using the QUAD recording system, a method of compressing four separate camera images onto a single frame, so that the guard can see all four views on one monitor screen and record them on a VCR at the same time. Digital TV also allows more frames on a single cassette, because digital compression technology reduces the amount of tape needed to record an image. These systems allow detailed surveillance and plant monitoring, so that guards can observe everything happening within a facility.[1]

There's no escape from this. Previously, you might have been under video surveillance at the entrance, but now, it's possible to watch you everywhere you go and to track you as you tour a facility. Using hard discs instead of videotape allows keeping a record of several months' worth of time-lapse video.

Cameras are much more sophisticated today than years ago. New circuits allow the camera to ignore bright, light-emitting objects within their fields of view. Miniaturization allows easier concealment. While deterrence is still one purpose of CCTV, seeing a camera merely persuades a criminal to transfer his activities to another part of the premises. Infra-red cameras allow surveillance in darkness.[2]

**Figure Seven**
*This CCTV camera photographs all vehicles entering a secure mobile home park. This didn't prevent a series of recent mail thefts.*

Video surveillance is portable, as well. The old days of concealing a camcorder in a briefcase or duffel bag have given way to subminiature cameras concealed in neckties and other items. Decoy items (items containing the surveillance equipment) include baseball caps, belt buckles, briefcases, eyeglasses, and wristwatches.[3]

We find CCTV in retail stores, airports, bus stations, railroad stations, subway stations, seaports, and other public and private locales. Their use is more extensive than what's immediately obvious. Police in some locales use CCTV cameras to observe busy roads and intersections and detect traffic bottlenecks. British police use CCTV cameras to scrutinize city streets as an "anti-crime" measure. The city of Montreal uses

CCTV cameras on bridge approaches to monitor road traffic and help authorities switch traffic control signals to keep vehicles moving. CCTV cameras also monitor unmanned toll booths elsewhere to let police spot those who go through without paying. Tunnels are often too cramped for live patrols, and CCTV allows police to identify problems such as fires and accidents as they occur.[4]

In many cases, police or security officers monitor the CCTV cameras. Retail stores employ security officers to watch for shoplifters, and real-time monitoring is essential if the officers are to react immediately and apprehend the offenders. When immediate action is necessary, reviewing a videotape hours after the event is useful only for evidence.

Crime control and deterrence are part of the picture. Police and security officers use CCTV to monitor parking garages, subway stations, and other public and private places to counter vandals, muggers, and thieves. These are under 24-hour surveillance, and officers respond whenever they see an occurrence.

In other cases, the purpose of CCTV and a recorder is to provide a record of events, not necessarily for immediate action, but as an inexpensive way to document events. Miniature TV cameras and slow-speed recorders provide 24-hour-a-day automatic surveillance. ATM machines and banks employ these for protection against robbery.

In many cases, the VCR is not located next to the camera. One reason is that there often isn't room for it in the enclosure. Another is that it's often desirable to have a central monitoring location serving dozens or

*Chapter Eight
Tools and Techniques*
79

hundreds of TV cameras. With video monitors and tape recorders, one officer can oversee a wide area, for greater efficiency.

Still another reason is to preserve equipment and tapes from destruction. When armed suspects robbed a video rental store in Albuquerque, New Mexico, in 1996, they were aware that security cameras were on the premises. After killing three clerks, they found the VCR and removed the tape. Robbers who killed the manager of an Albertson's supermarket in Albuquerque in 1997, however, were not as astute, and police had a videotape of the murder.

With the current concern over terrorism, preserving equipment and tapes is an important design feature. In London, critical central city areas are under constant TV surveillance because of the prospect of IRA bombs. When a 1,000 lb. bomb exploded in London's Docklands, several surveillance cameras caught the action. Commander John Grieve, head of Scotland Yard's anti-terrorist branch, stated that several cameras had picked up the events when terrorists parked their bomb-laden truck at the scene. Although the blast destroyed several cameras, their signals fed into remote recorders. "We have got a lot of good closed-circuit TV footage," Grieve said.[5]

A major manufacturer of low-profile CCTV cameras is Burle, and a model currently advertised is the Auto-Dome, an 8.5"-diameter black dome designed to "reduce losses while protecting profits." (Advertisement, *Security Management*, December, 1994, p. 9.) This motorized, remote-controlled camera rotates 360 degrees, tilts up and down, and zooms in on whatever the guard operating it finds interesting. There's even a choice of camera models; black-and-white, color, or high-resolution color. The system's sophisticated electronics keep the picture upright when a person walks right under the dome and to the other side. The camera rotates to maintain its up-and-down orientation.

One company that supplies an array of video surveillance equipment, including a smoke-detector camera, pinhole board camera, and recorders, is:

Security Products International, Inc.
30 Old Budd Lake Road
Budd Lake, NJ 07828
Phone: (201) 426-0800
Fax: (201) 426-0500
e-mail: SECPRO@1X.netcom.com

With extended-time video recorders, it's possible to have full-time surveillance. Sanyo produced the Model SRT-612DC, a VCR that provides 24-hour recording at ten frames per second. The Sanyo TLS-7000 provides 960-hour high-resolution recording for time-lapse surveillance. These are available from:

Sanyo
21605 Plummer Street
Chatsworth, CA 91311
Phone: (818) 998-7322, Ext. 286
Fax: (818) 717-2719

Cameras may be hidden or out in the open. Those displayed prominently are more for deterrence. Some

## Chapter Eight
## Tools and Techniques

models even have a red light to show that they're purportedly in operation. These are often dummies, for deterrence only. Genuine CCTV cameras are installed in a more low-key manner. They may be in ceiling enclosures, which don't fool anyone, but conceal the camera to minimize obtrusiveness. Some are even disguised as something else, such as a smoke detector. One model for mobile surveillance is disguised as a car radio antenna, and is waterproof.

Police are making increasing use of CCTV cameras. If you get stopped for a traffic offense, there may be a TV camera pointing at you from the police car. Today, an increasing number of police vehicles carry CCTV cameras aimed forward through the windshield. The camera is connected to a VCR in the vehicle's trunk. These provide documentation of vehicle pursuits and citizen contacts during traffic and felony stops. The police consider this important because some offenders claim police misconduct, and without a camera recording the action there's only the officer's word against the suspect's. The camera also shows the citizen's conduct, and records if the citizen staggered, struck the officer, etc.

The officer carries a radio microphone on his person to provide a sound track to accompany the video record. This provides an objective record of any conversation, to document any statements made. Thus, slurred speech can support a charge of drunk driving.

An officer can also carry a CCTV camera on his person. The COPCAM is a miniaturized camera and microphone attached to the front of the officer's shirt or jacket to record everything he sees. Transmitting the scene back to a recorder in the patrol vehicle, it allows the officer to record verbatim witness accounts, accident scenes, sobriety tests, and record a fleeing or assaultive suspect.

The COPCAM is sold by:

SEMCO Law Enforcement Products
1430 Vantage Court
Vista, CA 92083-8596
Phone: (800) 995-0636 Ext. 188

There's another way in which they're watching you. The 35mm camera is useful for another high-tech application: Photo-Radar. This is a camera and electronic flash connected to a speed radar set placed at the side of a road to automatically capture on film anyone exceeding the speed limit. The radar set measures the speed of each approaching vehicle, and the camera photographs the driver and front license plate of the speeding vehicles. The electronic flash lights up the inside of the vehicle to show the driver's face clearly. If the Photo-Radar is in use in a state requiring only a rear license plate, such as Arizona, a second camera photographs the vehicle as it recedes. After the film is developed, the police send a citation by mail to the vehicle owner. If the owner denies having been the driver, the photograph can either place him behind the wheel or the police can require the owner to identify who had the vehicle that day.

Although Photo-Radar is perfectly legal, many motorists feel that it's somehow unfair to be ticketed by a robot instead of a live police officer. This has provoked resentment.[6]

## Audio Surveillance

Watch what you say. It may be recorded and used against you.

Audio surveillance is no longer merely an arcane art practiced by spies and private detectives. Today, it's common-place, and spreading.

Tape recorders are a fact of life, and they're often used to document a transaction but not, as they'd have you believe, for the customer's protection. They are used for other purposes. When you telephone some companies and some government agencies, you hear a recording that says something like this:

"This transaction is being recorded to help us assure quality service to our customers."

This is as silly as the signs in one supermarket chain that required customers writing checks to leave their thumb prints on the checks. Signs announcing the new policy began: "FOR YOUR PROTECTION."

The real purpose of tape recording conversations is to check how efficiently employees handle them, how many they handle an hour, and to have evidence in case the customer says something that can be used against him.

Many police agencies now require their officers to carry tape recorders on their belts, and to record all public contacts, from traffic tickets to family disputes and criminal interrogations. Experience has shown that it's easier to get a conviction if the officer has a subject's damaging admissions on tape. The other side of it is, of course, that some members of the public stopped by an officer for an offense charge abuse by the officer, and the tape recording provides solid evidence regarding whether the alleged abuse did, in fact, take place.

When responding to a family dispute, officers will often try to separate the parties and interview them apart to get their versions of the affray. If you're involved in one of these, avoid using profanity during the heat of the moment. Your words played to a judge or jury will count against you.

You have to be really careful when you've done nothing wrong, but are the subject of an interview by a police officer. If, for example, you shoot an intruder in your home, you may have done so in perfect self-defense. However, be careful what you say and how you say it. If, for example, the intruder was a minority member and you use a disparaging term for the intruder, it will be on the tape. While it's not illegal to call someone a disparaging name, the attorney for the criminal or his survivors may find it grounds to launch a civil lawsuit against you. The lawyer knows that he's got a good chance of using that tape to convince a jury that you're merely a bigot seeking an excuse to shoot a minority person. Your own words can hang you.

It's significant that when there's a police-involved shooting, the detectives assigned to investigate often do not use a tape recorder because they know that, in the stressful aftermath of a violent event, the officer may blurt out something he later wishes he hadn't said. Therefore, they give him a chance to compose his thoughts before interviewing him for the record.

## Chapter Eight
## Tools and Techniques

Don't expect a fair shake from the cops, even if you're totally innocent. Their mind-set is that everyone is a suspect, and everyone lies. As we've seen earlier in this volume, they have ways of extorting confessions from innocent persons.

Keeping these facts in mind, the best action for you to take when interviewed by police regarding something that may produce a criminal charge against you is to say nothing, or as little as possible, and ask for legal counsel. You're required to identify yourself, but at that point, ask to speak with your lawyer. Don't take the officer's word for it that, since you've done nothing wrong, you have nothing to fear. Zip your lip. If the officer tries to whipsaw you by saying that only guilty parties have something to hide, continue to keep your mouth shut, except to ask for your lawyer again. Remember that a fish wouldn't get caught if he kept his mouth shut.

If you ever end up behind bars, you'll probably get your one phone call, but odds are that it will be recorded. Prison officials worry about inmates hatching plots and communicating them to accomplices outside. This is why they often use electronic equipment to record all telephone conversations. Some of these are between lawyer and client, but it doesn't matter — they all go onto tape. It depends on the ethics of the guards whether they listen in or not.

There are high-tech voice recorders that put every conversation on a CD disc. A model made for correctional use is the "Lazer Voice," using optical disk voice recording. This is supplied by:

Schlumberger Technologies, Inc.
3501 Holiday Drive, Suite #405
New Orleans, LA 70114
Phone: (800) 371-5716
Fax: (504) 362-3649

Americans are under increasing routine surveillance, but this doesn't necessarily mean that covert surveillance no longer exists. Police and internal security agencies such as the FBI, NSA, etc., use covert audio surveillance techniques for recording conversations otherwise not accessible to them. Telephone tapping still exists, and there is good reason it's more common today than before. With today's Electronic Switching Systems (ESS) it's no longer necessary to go out and physically tap a person's telephone line. It takes place in the central office, and it's absolutely undetectable.

Of course, wiretapping laws are stricter today than they've ever been, but enforcing them is another matter. There also exist some loopholes that allow national security agencies to tap telephones almost at will. In Washington, DC, there exists a "National Security Electronic Surveillance Court" that issues warrants for various sorts of electronic surveillance. It meets in camera, and the subject of the surveillance never knows that a tap on him has been authorized. An FBI agent will present an affidavit for a warrant, and typically the judge will grant it. This makes it perfectly legal.

The illegal side is impossible to measure because by necessity it's undocumented and secret. A police officer who wants to tap someone's phone must approach the local telephone company's security officer, who is usually a retired police officer or FBI agent, or otherwise formerly connected to law enforcement. The procedure is the same whether the tap is legal or unauthorized. In theory, the security officer must see a warrant before allowing a tap, but in practice, the "old boy network" sometimes takes the place of a legally executed warrant.

A private investigator must follow the same procedure, but his chances of obtaining a warrant for a telephone tap are poor to non-existent, because in most jurisdictions wiretapping is reserved strictly for official agencies. This is where networking comes into play again. A private investigator develops a network of contacts who can help him in his work. The security officer may be doing a favor for a friend, or merely doing it for a bribe, but the result is the same. The subject gets a tap on his line, completely without his knowledge.

There also exist electronic devices for "bugging" a room, motor vehicle, or other premises. One is the "tube mike," a plastic tube passed through a small hole in a wall to conduct sound from a room to a small microphone at the other end. This is "non-access surveillance," in FBI parlance.[7]

Tube microphones come in all sizes. Some are relatively large plastic tubes about ½" in diameter, but for tight spaces or maximum concealment there are "needle microphones," passed through cracks in doors and windows.

Another device is the "contact microphone," a piezo-electric crystal glued to a wall. This is the modern electronic version of the glass pressed against a wall to hear sounds in the next room.[8]

Contact mikes are somewhat more difficult to use, because they pick up all vibrations in the wall. Thus, if the microphone is attached to a wall near an elevator shaft, it will pick up the noise of the elevator. Other sounds, such as the rumble of traffic or even a subway train nearby, will also affect it. Water pipes also produce sounds in walls, and the resulting "white noise" can drown out any conversation.

If the agent has access to a room, he can plant a bug almost anywhere, even in the subject's clothing. Radio mikes transmit whatever they pick up to a nearby transmitter, eliminating the need for tell-tale wires. Their only drawback, if they're totally self-contained, is battery life. Other models fit into wall plugs, and take their power from the house current.

One type of portable radio mike is the size and shape of a credit card, with a range of several hundred feet and a 30-hour battery life. Slipped into the breast pocket of the subject's jacket, it permits monitoring a conversation held outdoors. The value of this is that many people think it's impossible to overhear a conversation held on the street or in a park, and that walking will defeat any prospect of a bug planted nearby.

There are available on the open market several models of gimmicked telephones that use the built-in microphone to pick up any conversation in the room, even when the telephone is not in use.

## Voice and Word Pattern Recognition

Computer technology has evolved progressively over the decades, and during the 1970s rumors began to surface that the U.S. National Security Agency had a super-computer that could monitor all of the overseas telephone conversations emanating from within the United States and recognize those in which the agency had an interest by using voice patterns and key words. It's impossible to employ a staff large enough to listen to all telephone conversations, read all faxes, etc., so word recognition has to be computerized. If the computer recognizes a key word or phrase, it records and sets aside the entire conversation or message for scrutiny by a human agent.[9]

Since the early days of voice pattern recognition, computers have become more powerful and more compact, and now there are commercially available models that record and analyze telephone conversations. One overt application is in a correctional setting, where inmates discussing escape or drug deals are of interest to the authorities.

Protection against manual or computerized eavesdropping has been in use for many decades. We'll discuss this in the section on self-protection.

## Proximity Cards

Originally, electronic cards were substitutes for keys, which were too easy to reproduce. A metal key blank and a file were all that were necessary to duplicate a key, but more sophisticated equipment is necessary to duplicate even the simplest sort of electronic card.

The first type of electronic card used barium ferrite as magnetic material, with a pattern of magnetic dots embedded in the magnetic layer. This was a significant advance over punched cards that were relatively easy to duplicate. In the early 1970s, IBM produced magnetic stripe cards, which are still used in credit cards and are somewhat more secure. However, they're still too easy to forge and must pass through a magnetic stripe reader.

The advent of Application Specific Integrated Circuit (ASIC) technology during the early 1980s resulted in what quickly became known as the "smart card," which could hold a variety of codes and information to make misuse or duplication almost impossible. This was the first "proximity card," which did not require direct contact through a card reader.[10]

A tuned circuit embedded in the card responded to frequencies transmitted by the reader, returning a signal that would unlock a door. The signal could also identify the card holder, so that a central computer could monitor when the individual entered and left the premises.

The proximity card is basically a "transponder," an electronic device that replies to a radio signal that "interrogates" it. The extended range model doesn't require even placing it near the card reader, as it transmits to a receiver several feet away.[11]

One of the most sophisticated proximity cards is the "Microstamp," with a range of about ten feet or more, depending on the model. This allows tracking

*Chapter Eight*
*Tools and Techniques*
91

movements through a corridor 20 feet wide or even larger.[12]

A very basic form of the proximity card is the merchandise tag placed on expensive items by retailers. The check-out clerk neutralizes the tag by passing it over a magnetic field at the register. If not deactivated, the tag responds to radio waves at a special portal at the exit and sounds an alarm to alert store guards. We see these portals today in department stores and even supermarkets.

**Figure Eight**
*This electronic gate, through which all who enter or leave this supermarket have to pass, is designed to pick up emanations from electronic tags attached to high-value merchandise. Many retail stores today have such gates, not just jewelry and fur stores.*

Another model is designed for airline luggage handling. This radio frequency identification tag serves to match luggage with passengers. The counter attendant attaches the tag to a passenger's luggage, and initializes it with the passenger's number. A card reader at the aircraft reads each tag as baggage loaders place the luggage into the cargo bay, and sends a signal to reconcile the luggage with the passenger list at the central computer. When all luggage matches the passenger list, the aircraft can take off. However, if a piece of luggage doesn't have a corresponding passenger who has boarded, a red alert flashes and baggage handlers unload the piece of baggage.[13]

The proximity portal allows users to pass through a lobby or doorway with the card reader automatically sensing their cards, which may be inside a pocket or purse, and logging them as having entered the facility. One application extends the proximity card's usefulness by turning it into a tracking device. Proximity readers installed along the walls of a building allow tracking each card within the facility. If you're carrying one of these cards within a building so equipped, the central computer can sense exactly where you are at all times. There is a record of which work area you're in, when you leave, and where else within the building you may go. If you go to the cafeteria, the computer will log when you left your work station, how long it took you to get to the cafeteria, which route you took, how long you remained in the cafeteria, when you started back and by which route, and when you arrived back in your work area. Likewise if you went to the bathroom. The computer can record whether you went to the men's room or the ladies' room.

## Electronic Databases

The computer age has brought surveillance into a new era in which information about almost anybody is available to almost anyone. There are dozens of government databases containing information about almost every resident of the United States. Realistically, the only way to drop off the government's radar screen is to become a bum or bag lady, and even this isn't certain because of the possibility of arrest.

Financial records are gathered privately by several giant companies that specialize in this sort of information. These "credit reporting bureaus" purportedly maintain credit records, but in fact keep far more than credit information in their databases.

The federal government has also gotten into financial surveillance. The so-called "Bank Secrecy Act" of 1970 was anything but. Instead, it provided for reporting to the U.S. Treasury Department any cash transactions over $10,000. Another provision is that individuals carrying sums greater than $10,000 across the U.S. border must file a Currency Transaction Report (CTR) with the Treasury Department.

In 1984, an amendment to the U.S. Internal Revenue Code required businessmen to file Form 8300 whenever they received $10,000 cash in a transaction. The Annunzio-Wylie Money Laundering Act of 1992 resulted in banks being required to file a Suspicious Activity Report (SAR) on "suspicious activity" involving more than $5,000. These go to the Financial Crimes Enforcement Network (FinCEN) and into a computer. Within six months after the introduction of the SAR, FinCEN reported that 31,143 SARs had been filed.[14]

How many of these computerized reports actually resulted in criminal prosecution is speculative. One thing that is certain is that these tidbits of information will remain in government computers almost forever.

The Internet has proved to be a bountiful source of information to government and private investigators, and even curious private individuals. Finding an individual's telephone number takes only a few seconds after logging on to one of the locator services. It's important to note, though, that the quality of service varies sharply with price and accessibility.

The ordinary on-line service is no better than the phone book, and in some ways it's definitely worse. While ordinarily locator services purport to provide addresses, e-mail numbers, and telephone numbers for people throughout the United States, in reality there are serious limits. They do not provide unlisted numbers, for example. Most do not do "reverse searches," retrieving the person's name and address from the telephone number. One that does is "Infospace," located at:

>   http://www.infospace.com

There exist specialized databases available mainly to private investigators. These cull information from telephone directories, city directories, voter registration lists, business license records, motor vehicle registration records, and many other public and private records to provide a profile of the person being

*Chapter Eight
Tools and Techniques
95*

investigated. One company offering comprehensive information of this sort is:

DBT ONLINE
1-800-279-7710

DBT advertises that it can provide information starting with only a name or social security number. Information includes individual demographics, past and present addresses, corporations and businesses, phone numbers, neighbors, relatives, assets, etc.

Another database service is:

OPEN, Online Professional Electronic Network
1650 Lake Shore Drive, Suite 180
Columbus, OH 43204
Phone: 1-800-935-6736

OPEN provides motor vehicle records, criminal offense records, workers' compensation claims, Social Security number verification, and telephone/address records. These are gathered mainly for pre-employment background checks.

The telephone company and several private concerns sell CD-ROMs containing every listed telephone number in the country, but these have two drawbacks. First, they only contain listed numbers, not "unpublished" or "unlisted" numbers. What's the difference? According to U.S. West, a "non-listed" number is left out of the published directory but is still available from directory assistance. A "non-published" number isn't available either way. Of course, these numbers are still available to government agencies. Internet services, on the other hand, draw not only from telephone company listings, but other sources, such as voter registration lists, which contain registrants' telephone numbers. The other drawback is progressive obsolescence, as people move, die, change names, and otherwise make their listings obsolete. Every CD-ROM sold is out of date because of the lead time involved. By contrast, an Internet listing can be only seconds old, providing you're using the right service.

Some people use the Internet for legitimate purposes, such as locating friends and family members, but others have more sinister purposes. "Stalkers," those who track down and harass people they dislike, are also out there. Some stalkers are "lovesick" stalkers, seeking penpals and romance on the Internet, and playing diabolical pranks on those who rebuff them.

Stalkers use a variety of dirty tricks to harass their victims. Some "SPAM" them, sending many meaningless messages, or providing their names to commercial interests that send out SPAM. There's a variety of dirty tricks to use, and these are the electronic equivalent of writing your name and phone number on toilet walls. Many sites have forums and meeting place pages, and it's easy to place an ad for sado-masochistic play, for example, and leave the victim's e-mail address. This takes advantage of the multiplier effect, because one ad can generate many responses. If the stalker has even a rudimentary knowledge of his "audience," he can write very enticing ads that will bring a lot of replies.

Others use the Internet to look up their victims' telephone numbers, and place crank calls using the conventional telephone system. Whatever the motive, stalking can make life pretty unpleasant for victims.

## Transmitter Location

Do you have a cellphone? Do you think nobody can tell where you are when you use it?

The science of locating radio transmitters began during World War I, when British direction-finding stations took bearings on German naval transmitters and plotted them to find the locations of German ships at sea. World War II saw great refinements in this field, as counterspies used radio direction-finding to locate enemy spies' transmitters. Since the end of that conflict, the Cold War has stimulated radio direction-finding, and technological developments have made finding a transmitter very quick and accurate.

There are basically three methods of finding a transmitter. The oldest is triangulation, in which several receiving stations with directional antennas take bearings on a transmission and communicate the bearings to a central plotting room. Technicians trace each bearing on a map of the area and the intersection of the bearings pinpoints the location of the transmitter.

The second method requires several receivers as well, and works by measuring the relative strengths of signals received. A computer analyzes the strengths and determines the location of the transmitter. The third method also requires a computer-controlled chain of receivers, and measures the minute differences in the time the signal arrives at each receiver.

Formerly classified, these techniques are now available on the civilian market for law enforcement and private security. One application is locating stolen cars by pinpointing radio transmitters installed in the vehicles for this purpose. Location of cellular phones is another application.

Police today are using this technology to pinpoint the location of cellphone users. A recent test run in New Jersey had encouraging results, from the police's point of view. Citizens dialing 9-1-1 had their calls routed to a tracing system that was designed to locate them with an accuracy within 410 feet at least 67 percent of the time. This was a live test, over a 100-day period, of a Federal Communications Commission mandate that police acquire the equipment to locate callers to the emergency number, 9-1-1. The federal mandate requires that the equipment be in place all over the country by October, 2001.[15]

Purportedly, this is to speed emergency response when a citizen calls for help. Many people cannot pinpoint their locations accurately enough when dialing 9-1-1, probably because they're unfamiliar with the geography of the area in which they're driving. Also, many drivers do not notice mileposts on freeways, and cannot identify their locations within a few miles.

Once the equipment is in place, it can, and will, serve other purposes. Criminal investigators will be able to pinpoint the location of a specific cellphone each time the caller uses it. This will help an investigation into a stolen cellphone, or help locate wanted persons unwise enough to use a cellphone.

## Chapter Eight
### Tools and Techniques

The more sinister aspect of this technology, though, is very obvious. Theoretically, the technology can locate every cellphone in the country every time someone makes a call on it. Experience has shown that every time new technology comes about for surveillance, both police and private security embrace it with enthusiasm, to keep tighter control of the people they're watching. We've seen this happen with CCTV, and we'll soon see it happening with cellphone locator technology.

One company advertising direction-finding equipment to the security industry is:

Doppler Systems, Inc.
P.O. Box 2780
Carefree, AZ 85377
Phone: (602) 488-9755
Fax: (602) 488-1295

Doppler Systems advertises that its fixed-site direction finders provide an accuracy within two degrees, and the company provides computer software for triangulation from a central control location. Doppler Systems also provides mobile versions covering 50MHz to 1GHz.

Doppler Systems use a sophisticated type of direction-finding antenna. Normally, a direction-finder will use a "directional" antenna, which varies in sensitivity depending on its orientation to the target signal. This system uses a rotating antenna, based on the principle that an antenna arm moving towards the target will show an increase in signal frequency, and the one moving away will show a decrease. This is the well-known "Doppler effect," which we know from common experience occurs when an emergency vehicle comes towards us. As long as the vehicle is moving towards us, the siren seems higher in pitch. Once it passes and begins moving away, the siren seems to drop to a lower note.

Another direction finder offered by Doppler is the Series 6100 mobile unit, designed to be mounted in a car. This uses an antenna unit mounted on the roof in a low-profile enclosure, connected to a laptop computer inside the vehicle. The unit's software provides a Line Of Bearing (LOB) that the user can plot on a digital map. A Global Positioning System (GPS) receiver provides the unit's location on the map. With the first bearing in the computer, the user drives to another location to take a second bearing, which also registers on the map. The transmitter's location is where the lines intersect.

In practice, the direction finder can be used in a pursuit, because the unit will show if the bearing is ahead of the mobile unit. Thus, the user can follow a person using a transmitter from a vehicle. In heavy traffic, though, identifying the actual vehicle is difficult.

Another device, sold only to police, is the "Cellphone ESN Reader," which reads the number of the targeted cellphone. This detects and records the cellular phone number, called number, and ESN of a target phone at ranges of up to two miles. The company providing this device is:

Curtis Electro Systems
4345 Pacific Street
Rocklin, CA 95677
Phone: (800) 332-2790
Fax: (916) 632-0636

Only police can buy this commercially produced scanner, but black-market models are available to criminals, who station themselves in high-traffic areas such as freeways and airport parking lots. With their illicit scanners, they pick up the Electronic Serial Number (ESN) and the Mobile Identification Number (MIN) of cellphones nearby, clone them into cellphones, and sell them.[16]

There's even a "Cellular Telephone Immobilizer" available to prevent you from using your cellphone. The ostensible purpose is to prevent cellphone use during concerts, movies, lectures, hospitals, where allegedly cellphone use is disturbing to performers or dangerous to other equipment. The system is a jammer, designed to work on all cellphone frequencies, disrupting the two-way full duplex link between cellphones and local cells. This makes it impossible for cellphones within range to transmit or receive. Range of the jammer is up to 200 meters, depending on power output, which runs from 10 mW to 1000mW.[17]

## E-mail

They're watching you and your e-mail at work. Don't assume that personal messages you send over your company's e-mail system are private. They're not, and court decisions have held that they're not. Let's look at actual cases:

One company's management became very disturbed when a casual look at its e-mailings revealed that one employee sent ethnic jokes on e-mail. Materials labeled "sexist" circulated among the staff.[18]

Company management was running scared, because such messages could lead to lawsuits, given today's politically correct and litigious atmosphere. E-mail can be evidence in a lawsuit when the plaintiff claims that he or she is in a "racist" or "sexist" workplace.

The net result is that you cannot expect your workplace e-mail messages to be read only by the addressee. A *Security Management* survey during 1996 showed that 67 percent of responding companies warned employees not to expect e-mail privacy. Fifty-two percent scanned e-mail during active investigations on specific matters. Thirty-eight percent periodically monitored e-mail content. Thirty-nine percent routinely monitored e-mail traffic.[19]

One policy tells employees that their e-mail will be monitored, and that accepting employment constitutes consent. Company policy can be Draconian at times. One company employee was the e-mail administrator and trainer, who had been told that e-mail was private, and who passed this on to those she trained. One day, her supervisor asked her to help him monitor employees' e-mail. She refused to help, and management fired her. She sued, but lost, because the court upheld the company's right to scrutinize employees' e-mail.[20]

Another, similar case had a kindred result. An employee, who had been assured that e-mail was private and would not be used as grounds for discipline or termination, found himself fired for sending alleged threats. He sued. However, the employer was successful in getting the suit dismissed.

That was in 1996. It's a safe assumption that companies will keep an increasingly watchful eye on their internal e-mail, and scrutinize what employees are saying to each other. Scrutinizing e-mail can easily have more than one benefit for a company. Originally instigated to avoid liability, reading employees' e-mail can also serve to alert management of dishonesty, disloyalty, and union activity. As we've seen, the original purpose may have been something else, but current use can be directed against union organizers and individual employees.

## Miscellaneous Bugging Devices

There are a wide variety of electronic surveillance devices available, a surprising number of them on the open market. Kits to install audio surveillance are available at retail and by mail-order, in the guise of crib surveillance devices. The parent who wants to know when a baby cries in another room can install the transmitter, which picks up all sounds in the baby's room. The receiver goes in the kitchen or elsewhere, and receives any cries the baby emits.

Specialty stores sell more advanced and miniaturized devices. Others are available via mail-order or from special suppliers. Some equipment is off-limits to any but police or well-connected private investigators.

Inspired amateurs can, of course, construct their own equipment. Surveillance technology is spreading, and some of it is inevitably directed at you.

## Notes:

1. Newton, Mike, "Picturing The Future of CCTV, *Security Management,*" November, 1994, pp. 60-63.
2. Radke, Mark G., "Piecing Together The CCTV Picture," *Security Management*, September, 1996, pp. 113-117.
3. Gips, Michael A., "Tie Spy," *Security Management*, November, 1996, pp. 20-21.
4. O'Brien, Jim, "CCTV Watches The World Go By," *Security Management*, June, 1992, pp. 27A-28A.
5. Darbyshire, Nigel, Johnston, Phillip, Jones, George, and Fenton, Ben, "Video Hunt For Lorry Bombers," London, *The Daily Telegraph*, February 12, 1996, p. 1.
6. Harman, Alan, "Speed Cameras Cause Controversy," *LAW and ORDER*, July, 1997, p. 67.
7. *The Whole Spy Catalog*, Lapin, Lee, San Mateo, CA, Intelligence Incorporated, 1995, p. 274.
8. *Ibid.*, p. 276.
9. *Ibid.*, p. 267.
10. Clarke, Barry, "Get Carded With Confidence," *Security Management*, November, 1994, pp. 78-84.
11. *Ibid.,* p. 82.
12. Advertisement for Micron, *Security Management*, September, 1996, p. 57.

13. Chunn, Sherri, "LANL Spin-off Firm May Make Skies Safer," *Albuquerque Journal*, August 4, 1997, Business Outlook, p. 1.
14. Horowitz, Richard, "The Low Down on Dirty Money," *Security Management*, October, 1997, pp. 50-53.
15. "Cellular E-911 Technology Gets Passing Grade in NJ Test," *Law Enforcement News*, July/August, 1997, p. 5.
16. Shannon, Elaine, "Reach Out And Waste Someone," *Time Digital*, July/August, 1997, p. 36.
17. SPY Electronics, http://w972.com/spy/spy456.htm.
18. Thompson, Amy, and Harowitz, Sherry, "Taking A Reading on E-Mail Policy," *Security Management*, November, 1996, pp. 55-56.
19. *Ibid.,* p. 57.
20. Trickey, Fred L., "E-Mail Policy By The Letter," *Security Management*, April, 1996, p. 70.

# Chapter Nine
# The Internet

The controllers in legislatures and police agencies are always seeking excuses to broaden their powers and impose new restrictions on the people in their jurisdictions. One recent textbook case is the Internet.

The Internet, which began as a computer communication network between universities and laboratories decades ago, has turned into a vast public forum accessible to anyone with a computer. Quite logically, criminals have made use of it, as they'll exploit any technological innovation. Also quite logically, federal and local law enforcement have put their fingers into the pie, for obvious reasons.

Criminals are often ahead of the power curve, leaving police far behind and hoping to catch up eventually. One type of criminal activity that has made wide use of computer networks is the organized child molestation ring. During the early 1980s a number of sexually-oriented computer bulletin boards sprang up, connected by telephone lines and modems.[1]

Several organizations devoted to pedophilia and pederasty made quick use of computers for networking, and several more ad hoc groups sprang up as well. Among the more traditional groups are the Rene Guyon

Society and the North American Man-Boy Love Association (NAMBLA). There are also informal "chat rooms" devoted to sexual as well as other topics. These are where child molesters meet on-line, and exchange information about their deeds because some read the accounts for sexual stimulation. Molesters trade descriptions and addresses of victims, and cooperate in other ways over the Internet.

Police reaction is obvious, if often delayed. Undercover police agents will join chat rooms and try to obtain investigative leads. These include identities of participants, identities and descriptions of possible victims, descriptions of illegal acts, and other information useful for building a case.

One investigator who has developed a knack for this type of investigation is Detective Daryl Rowland, of the Huntington Beach, CA, Police Department. Rowland trolls for pedophiles by cruising the chat rooms, posing as one of them or as a potential victim. He adopts several personas, such as that of a young man seeking photos of minors, a father who molests his son, and a 13-year-old boy exploring the chat rooms. In one case, Rowland enticed a 39-year-old Allentown, PA, man to come to Huntington Beach to have oral sex with Rowland's nonexistent 12-year-old son.[2]

Federal agencies monitor on-line providers as well. The U.S. Secret Service obtained a court order to monitor one man's electronic mail on CompuServe, and developed evidence for an arrest on a charge of conspiring to sell illegal electronic equipment. The FBI obtained America OnLine (AOL)'s cooperation in monitoring some subscribers suspected of transmitting child pornography, and obtained evidence to support arrests.[3]

Two problems seriously obstruct investigations. One is that most participants use "handles," or aliases, to protect their identities. The other is that descriptions of sex acts encountered by investigators may be fantasies, not real-life accounts. Despite these problems, investigators can still develop useful information from chat room accounts. Such investigative leads can include locales where molesters prey on children, methods they use to entice children to cooperate, and various personal details that can lead to identifying some molesters.

Federal censorship attempts were inevitable. The government has already tried to ban pornography from the Internet. This was only a way of sticking a foot into the door, although it was shot down by the U.S. Supreme Court. However, federal agencies are making a serious effort to tap into everything passing through the Internet, partly because organized crime and drug rings exchange information on the wires.

FBI Director Louis Freeh made a bid for a law restricting data encryption programs and devices, to allow federal agencies to decode messages on the Internet. Freeh stated before the Senate Judiciary Committee that child molesters, purveyors of child pornography, and drug traffickers are using encryption to frustrate investigators. Freeh's solution was that all encryption systems should have "keys" to decode them, available to law enforcement officials.[4]

Private enterprises are eager to exploit the Internet as a marketing tool. The "cookies" planted in Internet users' hard drives, listing their preferences and surfing patterns, are well known. More recently, AOL had to abandon plans to provide members' telephone numbers to telemarketing firms after both members and New York State Attorney General Dennis Vacco objected.5

The Internet is still developing, and we can only guess how both private and public agencies plan to use it for surveillance in the future. In their zeal to prosecute criminals, law enforcement officers may turn all of us into potential suspects. Private agencies, especially those involved in marketing, view the Net as a golden opportunity to gather marketing information to sell to advertisers.

## Notes:

1. Rapp, Burt, *Sex Crimes Investigation*, Port Townsend, WA, Loompanics Unlimited, 1988, pp. 131-133.
2. "'Net Proceeds," *Law Enforcement News*, January 31, 1997, p. 4.
3. Trickey, Fred L., "E-Mail Policy By The Letter," *Security Management*, April, 1996, p. 71.
4. Burrell, Cassandra, "Lawmen Seek Key To Computer Criminals," Associated Press, July 10, 1997, *Albuquerque Journal*, p. 7.
5. Kalish, David E., "AOL Opts to Keep Phone Numbers," Associated Press, July 25, 1997, *Albuquerque Journal*, p. C-4.

# Chapter Ten
# Protecting Yourself

There are several steps you can take to protect yourself, but be aware that none is totally effective. Protection covers two areas: active and passive. Active methods mean specific actions you take to protect yourself and your privacy. Passive methods are acts of omission, avoiding certain behaviors that draw attention to you. Let's begin by considering a passive measure:

## Shopping Defense

You can protect your privacy by avoiding shopping at supermarkets that pressure you into signing up for their in-house discount cards. We've seen how these are just stratagems for building up a profile of customers, which the markets then sell to advertisers. If you stick to markets that don't have such cards, you'll probably save money as well, because their prices tend to be lower.

## Fan Letters

Many people write adulatory letters to media people they admire. A few, very few, are mentally disturbed persons who may escalate into stalking or even violence. This is why many media people have secret addresses, do not receive mail at home, and even have their phones and utilities listed in their employer's or attorney's names.

*CNN*, the Cable News Network, has a security policy that all fan letters to its personnel must go to the security department. The letter writer goes into a computerized file, and this means that if you write a letter to one of the news people at *CNN*, your name and address will be on a computer disk.

If the letter writer sends more than one letter, and someone in the security department suspects this person may be vaguely threatening, he sends a form letter to the writer, explaining that all letters are read by the security department.[1]

The lesson is clear. Write a letter to, or even try to telephone a TV news reader and you'll fall under suspicion of being a weirdo. This is typical of security people, who try to magnify the importance of their very dull, routine jobs by treating everyone as a suspect and potential threat. The countermeasure for you is very simple. Don't attempt to contact media people, even for a friendly chat. They don't view it that way, because the suspicious attitude infects them and they see members of their public as threats, or just nuisances.

Letters to politicians are often futile. If your local representative takes enough interest to answer his mail, you may have an impact. However, letters to the president often go unanswered, or you may get a stock reply on White House stationery assuring you that the president just loves to hear from citizens, and will take your views into consideration. This is laughable, but the odds are good that your letter will result in your name ending up in a computer file maintained by the U.S. Secret Service, the agency that takes a keen interest in people who write to the president, especially if they feel there's something kooky about your letter.

If you hold minority views, such as those expressed by fringe groups, you'll be in a file for sure. If ever there is legislation banning such groups, you'll be on a suspect list.

## Making Driver's Licenses Work For You

Although today driver's licenses are for practical purposes national I.D. cards, there are ways to liberate yourself from the net. Forgery of a license is difficult, and getting more so, because technology is producing driver's licenses that are increasingly hard to forge. Another problem is "backstopping," which is having a record in the motor vehicle bureau if a police officer stops you and checks out your license by radio. Even if you have a perfectly forged license, you'll be in trouble when the message comes back to the officer that there's no record of such a license at the motor vehicle bureau.

Even an expired license won't get you into much trouble. The officer may or may not make an issue of it, and the worst that can happen is receiving a citation for driving with an expired license.

# They're Watching You!
The Age of Surveillance

The key is to have genuine driver's licenses from several different states. It's a simple, step-by-step process. First, obtain a duplicate license from your home state's motor vehicle bureau, saying that your original was lost or stolen. Next, when you visit another state, go to its motor vehicle bureau to obtain a license from that state. Chances are that you won't have to go through the entire process again. You'll merely have to turn in your out-of-state license.

However, to obtain a driver's license, you must furnish a resident address within that state. It must be a street address, as they won't accept a post office box. There are at least two ways to set up a street address where you can also receive mail such as license renewal forms. One is to use the address of a friend or relative within that state. Another is to rent a box at a mail receiving service, or mail drop. The mail drop must receive mail at its street address, not at it own post office box. Be very clear about this before you sign the contract and hand over the rent.

You turn in the original, trading it for a new license from the other state. Now you have two licenses, both genuine, and both in your name.

You use one license to obtain vehicle insurance. This is the one you keep pristine, and never show to a police officer who stops you for a traffic offense. The other license is the sacrificial one on which you can accumulate points because this one won't affect your insurance premiums. Even if it's an expired license, you're not in much trouble, as we've seen. Another point is that cops usually don't make much of an issue of it if your driver's license is from one state and your

## Chapter Ten
### Protecting Yourself

vehicle is registered in another. You can always explain that your mother, who lived in another state, just died and you re-registered her vehicle in your name at the nearest motor vehicle office.

"Jeff" used several driver's licenses, but in a creative way, adding a couple of wrinkles to make his system more flexible and foolproof. One problem he overcame is the increasing tendency of states to cross-check driver's licenses via computer. For example, when he tried to renew his genuine Arizona driver's license, the clerk behind the counter informed him that he had an active license in Florida. The two states compare records to prevent stunts of this sort.

The motor vehicle bureau makes its comparisons by name and date of birth. This is why Jeff tries to change one letter of his name or one digit of his date of birth each time he applies for another license. If the clerk doesn't notice that the applicant's license says "02/13/41" and the application for the new one says "02/14/41" he's home free. The new license will be genuine, but will not correlate with any others in the computer database.

Jeff found that certain states present more problems than others. Florida, for example, requires proof of your Social Security number before issuing a driver's license. This is an additional security check, and makes it almost impossible to obtain another driver's license in Florida if you already have a license in the states with which the Florida Department of Motor Vehicles maintains a computer link.

Jeff also found that he was able to register his Volvo in California, although he had an Arizona driver's license at the time. It's a mystery why the California Department of Motor Vehicles did this, but one possible explanation is that they're more interested in collecting revenue than following procedure.

There are other advantages to having a driver's license in certain states. Texas and Nevada, for example, do not have state income taxes. Establishing your legal residence in one of these states often exempts you from having to pay state income tax where you work or spend most of your time. An exception is a state such as Arizona, where simply holding a job in that state makes you a legal resident and subject to its state income tax.

If you earn income by investments, fees, or another way that is not geographically linked, you can still live in one state that has income tax, earn income, and have an income tax-free state as your legal residence. Also, many retirees establish legal residences in states without income taxes, collect Social Security by direct deposit into an account within that state, and wander about the country in motor homes.

This shows that you can gain several advantages by having more than one driver's license, provided you go about it the right way. Of course, don't make the mistake of using your licenses for something overtly criminal, such as big-time fraud. Discretion is important, and that means keeping a low profile. Don't make waves and slip silently through the system, in order to make multiple driver's licenses work for you.

## Telephone Privacy

There is no way to make your telephone number absolutely inaccessible to others. It doesn't matter what precautions you take: there are ways of penetrating your security if someone tries hard enough.

First, let's recognize that having an "unlisted" number means nothing. Both government and private investigators can find out your number and where you live. The only way to have a truly invisible number is to acquire someone else's number. One possibility is renting a house or apartment with a telephone still operating. This isn't as easy as it seems, because most telephone subscribers will want to take their service with them.

Roger rented a house where the resident had just died. Renting it from her daughter, he stated that he would simply continue to pay the telephone bill, and save her the trouble of having the service disconnected. Roger thus ended up with a telephone listed in the name of a dead person, because none of the drones in the telephone company's accounting department ever questioned why he was paying the bills for the listed subscriber. Remember, the telephone company is mainly interested in collecting money, and everything else is a poor second-place priority. This is the flip side of the telephone company's indifference to telephone scam operators.

An important precaution if you have a truly private number is never calling an 800-, 888-, or 900-number. These capture your number, to allow listing it on the customer's bill. There is a technique of enticing people to call toll-free or pay-per-call numbers to capture the calling numbers, thus making this information available to private investigators. The trick is to send the subject a letter purporting to be from a law firm, and asking the subject to call their 800-number for information about an inheritance. If you must call a toll-free number, do so from a pay phone a few miles away from where you live.

Don't think that owning a cellular phone provides any sort of privacy. Remember the slow speed chase during which the Los Angeles Police Department pursued O.J. Simpson down the freeways? This was the result of radio direction-finding, which can pinpoint the location of any transmission within seconds. Transmitter location equipment can operate from fixed sites, but there are mobile models available as well, as we've seen.

Eavesdropping is definitely possible, because of the large number of scanners on cellphone wavelengths. Further production of scanners tuned to cellphone frequencies is prohibited by law, but there are enough pre-ban scanners that will pick up these frequencies. An extra hazard is black-market scanners and devices to capture your ESN.

Ultimately, the best protection is not to have a telephone at all. This can be inconvenient, but it avoids any electronic trail to you.

A pager is one way of maintaining your privacy because it's totally passive. It only receives, but does not transmit, making it impossible to locate. You give out your pager number to those who might want to contact you, and you return your pages from public phones.

When returning calls, even from public phones, keep in mind that although you're not traceable, the person you're calling might have a tap on his phone. Watch what you reveal.

With the advent of computerized voice-pattern recognition and word and phrase searching, there's even more need for precautions. If you think your voice pattern is in someone's computer database, never make a call without using a voice-alteration device. This will change some of the frequencies in your voice to make it much harder for a computer to pick you out of millions of other conversations.

The way to evade key word and phrase recognition is even easier, and much older: using cryptonyms. Using substitute words to avoid certain meaningful key words has been employed by criminals and others for many decades. If you're into making bombs or dealing drugs, for example, never use these words on the telephone. Instead, substitute "package" or "parcel." Use aliases during telephone conversations, in case someone's listening. Likewise for place names. Use "Phoenix" instead of "Cleveland." Keep a short list of code words on your person for use with people you regularly contact by phone.

If you have to mention a name you don't want to pronounce, but have no code name on your list, spell it out. A human operator would recognize the subterfuge, but computers are dumb, believe it or not.

## Bugging Defense

While it's unlikely that an official or private agent is going to place a bug in your bedroom, normal security precautions can reduce the odds even further. If you're intent on preserving your privacy, the first step is not letting anyone know where you live. Obviously they can't plant a bug if they don't know where to put it. Address privacy may be difficult if you hold a regular job, and impossible if you try to live a mainstream life, with a wife, kids in school, etc.

Of course, someone wanting to bug you could have you do his work for him. Planting a bug in your briefcase or lunch pail is one way of getting you to carry the bug into your home, thereby avoiding the need for breaking and entering. It may be tedious to search your briefcase and to go through your pockets every evening before going home, but if you feel you're the object of covert surveillance, it may be worth the trouble.

Another security tactic is to be suspicious of any parcels you receive. A lamp sent you as a "gift" may contain a microphone powered by house current. In this regard, it's worth remembering the great seal given to the American ambassador to Moscow by the Soviets just after World War II. This contained a microphone powered by microwaves beamed into the embassy from a nearby building. This bug remained operational for years, while American security agents puzzled over the Soviet knowledge of American plans. After ruling out other leaks, it became obvious that the Soviets could only have obtained this knowledge by bugging the embassy. Eventually they found it, after going over the ambassador's office with a finetooth comb.

## Computer Privacy

Be very careful if you're on the Internet. If you have kinky sexual habits that are illegal, be aware that there are undercover investigators such as Detective Rowland out there trolling for people such as yourself. Don't tell strangers of your proclivities. Just because someone in a chat room tells you that he enjoys sex with 12-year-old boys doesn't mean he really does. Take anything you read with a grain of salt, because undercover investigators are experts in enticing people into traps.

Also note that many bulletin boards, sites, and chat rooms carry warnings to users advising them to be very careful regarding any contacts made on the Internet. People can, and do, misrepresent themselves in order to gain an advantage over others. Never take any electronic persona at face value. The voluptuous blonde may be really a 14-year-old high-schooler playing games.

One protective measure is to conceal your identity inside a waterproof compartment, invulnerable to casual observation. Many people do not use their real names, instead using "handles," to avoid revealing themselves. This also pertains to e-mail. It's not necessary to have your real name in your e-mail address. Instead, you can use something like

"Realguy@hotbot.com," or "Realguy@12345.6789.compuserve.com." Nevertheless, keep in mind that government agencies can trace you despite this.

As we've seen, many Internet sites plant "cookies" on your hard drive. One way to protect yourself is to delete the "cookies.txt" file from your drive after every session on the net. If using Windows, bring up your file manager and locate the cookies file, which is usually on the net program directory. Delete it, and when you log on again, there won't be any cookies file to betray your previous activities.

Finally, you may encounter a stalker. Defense against stalkers is possible, despite the anonymity of the Internet. First, your stalker is likely to have a personal reason arising from his (or her!) contacts with you. A rejected suitor may have given you some personal details, such as his name and address. This can be helpful if you feel threatened enough to tell the police. Save all stalking or SPAM messages, print them out, and bring them with you when you go to the police.

Lesser steps are also workable. One way to stop junk messages is to send copies to the sender's Internet provider. Providers include CompuServe, NETCOM, etc. In some cases, you can e-mail them directly. For example, complaints to NETCOM should go to "abuse.NETCOM.COM."

Harassing phone calls are another matter. You can use Caller ID to discover the identity of someone who hangs up on you. An answering machine is even more helpful, because Caller ID does not show blocked calls. The answering machine screens the caller from you even if you're at home. Finally, some telephone companies have tracing services. U.S. West, for example, advises customers to use Call Rejection or Call Trace as defenses against unwanted calls. To activate Call Rejection, press "*60" and follow the instructions. To use Call Trace, press "*57" after every unwanted call. Then follow the recorded instructions. The telephone company's security department will take action after three unwanted calls from the same number. Of course, if the situation seems serious enough to notify police, do so immediately, and they'll obtain the name and address of the harassing caller from the telephone company and take appropriate action. Maybe.

Unfortunately, the telephone company will not disclose to you the identity of the unwanted caller. This is typical of its high-handed manner towards its subscribers.

## On The Job

Today, the workplace is more dangerous than before, not so much because of occupational safety problems, but because of the trend towards downsizing and increased employee surveillance. They're watching you, even before they hire you, and you must be prepared to pass a background check and probably some sort of psychological test as well in order to gain employment.

Once hired, be very discreet until you know the lay of the land. Resist the temptation to put even a pencil into your pocket until you know where all surveillance cameras are located. How do you find out? Simple: be your own undercover agent. Keep your eyes and ears open, and listen to what other employees say during lunch and coffee breaks. Old hands have probably been there when covert surveillance cameras were installed, and can probably point them out to you.

Company undercover agents are uncommon, because of the expense involved, but company spies seem to proliferate in some corporations. The corporate culture may be paranoid, encouraging such behavior. Snitches are employees who try to curry favor with the boss by informing. There's a double danger here, so beware of fellow employees who seem a bit too friendly, and a mite too eager to learn about your business. You'll learn to develop a "patter," conversation lines that tell people about yourself, but reveal only what you want them to know. Be loquacious about innocent topics, such as sports, and be aggressive about changing the subject if you feel you're being "pumped." Avoid relating any personal details that might be used against you later. If you have a relative in prison, for example, keep it to yourself. This can only count against you, in the eyes of a company security director.

Be especially careful if anyone tries to entice you into any sort of illegal activity. If, for example, you admitted to another employee that you once smoked marijuana, and he tries to persuade you to smoke a joint on or off company time, don't fall for it. It may be merely a friendly gesture, or it may be entrapment, but if you guess wrongly, you'll pay a heavy price for being a sucker.

If your company may be the target of industrial espionage, be especially careful and discreet. There will be security briefings by your employer's security director, and it's smart to listen closely because these will bring you up to date on the latest tricks.

Security rules will cover visitors, and it's wise not to try to smuggle any unauthorized persons, even relatives, into your workplace. You'll also want to be discreet about what you say regarding your work or your employer. The listener may be working for your rival, or may repeat your words to your employer's security director.

Avoid any gossip about fellow employees. Innocently saying "Ralph, over there, needs a lot of money because he's got his mother in a nursing home!" can do a lot of harm if it reaches the wrong ears. A rival's agent might approach Ralph and offer him a deal: money for secrets.

Do not answer any "blind" employment ads unless you really don't care about your job. Also, be careful what you say during any employment interview. Showing off your knowledge can be playing right into the hands of corporate spies who use these interviews to pick applicants' brains.

## E-Mail

They're watching you... if you're using your company's e-mail. You might be surprised at the reasons for their surveillance. After all, e-mail is harmless, isn't it? Well, that's not the way CEOs and security directors see it. This is the era of political correctness, whatever the First Amendment says. There are certain things you'd better not say aloud, or send over any wires. This is especially true if you're involved in anything illegal.

## Photo-Radar

Photo-Radar can trap you if you're exceeding the speed limit, especially if you're not attentive. However, the way police use Photo-Radar is unlike the way radar cops work. Unlike radar cops, there are usually signs posted at the side of the road that Photo-Radar is in use ahead, and it's worth remaining alert enough to see such signs. Once the flash fires, you're caught.

Some motorists haven't been willing to let it go at that. A British motorist (Yes, Photo-Radar is in wide use in other countries) who was caught in its flash returned with a rope, which he tied to the unit and drove away. Others have tried to remove the film, spray paint the lens, cover the cameras with plastic or canvas sheeting, and turn them in the wrong direction.[2]

Unfortunately, doing this can get you in worse trouble, because you've already been caught on film. Photo-Radar units are built to make removing the incriminating film very difficult. Unless you can remove the entire unit without being seen, your goose is cooked.

Still, there are defenses. One is to place a covering of transparent kitchen plastic film over your license plates. This will reflect the flash and cause a glare on the film where your license plate would have registered. Radar-reflective coverings are sold through mail-order catalogs. They are illegal in some states.

Another defense is using a standard radar detector, which will pick up the unit's radar emissions before you're close enough for them to reflect back to the unit. Be careful, though, because despite police denials, sometimes these units are just over the crest of a hill or around a bend, which means that you're suddenly right in the beam.

Another reason to be careful is that Photo-Radar has a very narrow angle, unlike many other police radars that send radiation in a wide arc, which inadvertently sets off radar detectors far away from the target area. Photo-Radar is typically focused on a very narrow stretch of road, and even on level ground you're less likely to pick it up long before you reach its effective range.

Self-protection is possible, but only if you understand how modern surveillance methods work and can use their weaknesses against them. Complete freedom from surveillance is impossible today, but you can appear invisible or at least unremarkable to those who are watching.

## Notes:

1. Gips, Michael A., "Security Anchors CNN," *Security Management*, September, 1996, pp. 46-55.
2. Harman, Alan, Speed Cameras Cause Controversy, *Law & Order*, July, 1997, p. 67.

# Chapter Eleven
# The Future

The future looks bleak because technological means, aided and abetted by both government and private agencies, are becoming more effective in helping the controllers to keep an eye on everyone in the country. Government regulations, for example, are making the notion of privacy obsolete. When the government can enforce an encryption standard, banning encryption methods the government code-breakers cannot read, your privacy is totally gone. Significantly, there have been several such bills introduced in Congress. If the government requires that all pagers emit a signal to allow government agents to trace them, pagers will become beacons betraying your whereabouts instead of tools to protect your location.

The government isn't the biggest threat, as we've seen from analyzing the trends. Surveillance equipment is big, big, business, expanding at a compound annual growth rate of 13.8 percent. This market should be about $4 billion by 2001, if current trends continue.[1]

The chameleon's protective technique seems to be the best hope for individualists. With everyone under surveillance, the best defense is to take advantage of the information overload this causes, and to avoid standing out from the crowd.

## Notes:

1. Bowman, Erik J., "Security Tools Up For The Future," *Security Management*, January, 1996, p. 30.

# YOU WILL ALSO WANT TO READ:

☐ **58080 THE PRIVACY POACHERS, How the Government and Big Corporations Gather, Use and Sell Information About You,** *by Tony Lesce.* This book explains how various snoops get their hands on sensitive information about you, such as your financial records, medical history, legal records and much more. This information is then packaged and sold, over and over again, without your consent. Find out what the Privacy Poachers have on you, and what you can do to protect yourself. *1992, 5½ x 8½, 155 pp, soft cover.* **$16.95.**

☐ **10065 HOW TO HIDE THINGS IN PUBLIC PLACES,** *by Dennis Fiery.* Did you ever want to hide something from prying eyes, yet were afraid to do so in your home? Now you can secrete your valuables away from home, by following the eye-opening instructions in this book, which identifies many of the public cubbyholes and niches that can be safely employed for this purpose. Absolutely the finest book ever written on the techniques involved in hiding your possessions in public hiding spots, profusely illustrated with over 85 photographs. *1996, 5½ x 8½, 220 pp, illustrated, soft cover.* **$15.00.**

☐ **10048 THE BIG BOOK OF SECRET HIDING PLACES,** *by Jack Luger.* This book tells how searchers find hidden contraband and how to hide your stuff so it can't be found. Topics include: Hiding places in the home and the automobile; Tools and techniques used by searchers including mirrors, metal detectors, vapor detectors, dogs and more!; The different types of searchers you may encounter and the intensity of the search they conduct; And much, much more. *1987, 8½ x 11, 128 pp, more than 100 illustrations, soft cover.* **$14.95.**

☐ **91085 SECRETS OF A SUPER HACKER,** *by The Knightmare.* The most amazing book on computer hacking ever written! Step-by-step, illustrated details on the techniques used by hackers to get at your data. No person concerned with computer security should miss this amazing manual of mayhem. *1994, 8½ x 11, 205 pp, illustrated, soft cover.* **$19.95.**

You can get these titles at your favorite book store, or contact any of our distributors (listed on the next page).

**Bookpeople**
7900 Edgewater Drive
Oakland, CA 94621
1-800-999-4650

**Homestead Books**
6101 22nd Avenue NW
Seattle, WA 98107
1-800-426-6777

**Ingram Book Company**
One Ingram Blvd.
La Vergne, TN 37086-1986
1-800-937-8000

**Last Gasp of San Francisco**
2948 20th St.
San Francisco, CA 94110
1-415-824-6636
Fax: 1-415-824-1836

**Left Bank Distribution**
1404 18th Avenue
Seattle, WA 98122
1-206-322-2868
jonkonnu@eskimo.com

**Marginal Distribution**
277 George Street N
Unit 102
Peterborough, Ontario
K9J 3G9
Canada
1-705-745-2326

**Van Patten Publishing**
19741 41st Avenue NE
Seattle, WA 98155
1-206-306-7187
Fax: 1-206-306-7188

**Loompanics Unlimited**
PO Box 1197
Port Townsend, WA 98368
1-800-380-2230
Fax: 1-360-385-7785